Table of Contents

Chapter 1: Introduction to Firebase

1.1 Understanding Firebase and Its Capabilities

Firebase is a comprehensive mobile and web application development platform provided by Google. It offers a wide range of tools and services to help developers build high-quality apps, improve user experiences, and grow their user base. Firebase is known for its ease of use, real-time capabilities, and scalability, making it a popular choice for both startups and established companies.

Firebase provides various services, each catering to different aspects of app development. Here, we will delve into the core capabilities of Firebase and what makes it a valuable asset for modern app development.

What is Firebase?

Firebase is a cloud-based platform that encompasses a set of products and services designed to simplify app development tasks and enhance app performance. It can be seen as a Backend as a Service (BaaS) and a Mobile Backend as a Service (MBaaS) platform, as it handles many server-side tasks and provides a backend infrastructure for mobile and web applications.

Firebase was initially developed as an independent company and was later acquired by Google. This acquisition has resulted in the integration of Firebase with other Google services, making it a seamless choice for developers who want to leverage the power of Google's infrastructure and analytics.

Key Firebase Capabilities

1. **Realtime Database**: Firebase's Realtime Database is a NoSQL, cloud-hosted database that allows developers to store and sync data in real-time. It's particularly useful for building collaborative applications, chat apps, and any app that requires synchronized data across devices.

2. **Authentication**: Firebase offers a robust authentication system, supporting various authentication providers like email/password, Google, Facebook, and more. It simplifies user management and helps you secure your app's data and resources.

3. **Cloud Firestore**: Firestore is Firebase's newer and more flexible NoSQL database. It allows for more complex queries, better scalability, and a richer data modeling experience. Firestore is often preferred for larger and more data-intensive applications.

4. **Firebase Storage**: Firebase Storage provides scalable cloud storage for user-generated content like images, videos, and files. It offers easy integration with other Firebase services and allows you to securely store and retrieve user-generated content.

5. **Firebase Hosting**: Hosting lets you deploy and host web applications quickly and easily. It supports static and dynamic content, offers SSL support, and can be used for single-page applications (SPAs) and progressive web apps (PWAs).

6. **Firebase Functions**: Firebase Functions is a serverless compute platform that allows you to run backend code without managing servers. You can use it to execute code in response to events, such as database changes or HTTP requests.

7. **Analytics**: Firebase Analytics provides insights into user behavior and engagement within your app. It helps you understand how users interact with your app, track events, and measure the impact of changes.

8. **Performance Monitoring**: Firebase Performance Monitoring helps you monitor the performance of your app. It provides data on app startup times, network latency, and other critical performance metrics.

9. **Cloud Messaging**: Firebase Cloud Messaging (FCM) allows you to send messages and notifications to users across different platforms, including Android, iOS, and web.

10. **Machine Learning**: Firebase integrates with Google's machine learning services, making it easier to add machine learning capabilities to your app, such as image recognition or natural language processing.

Why Choose Firebase?

Firebase is a popular choice for app development for several reasons:

- **Ease of Use**: Firebase's intuitive interface and documentation make it accessible to developers of all levels of expertise.

- **Real-time Capabilities**: Firebase's real-time database and Firestore enable developers to build responsive and collaborative applications with ease.

- **Scalability**: Firebase can scale with your app's growth, ensuring it can handle increased user loads and data demands.

- **Google Integration**: The platform seamlessly integrates with other Google services, such as Google Cloud Platform (GCP) and Google Analytics.

- **Authentication and Security**: Firebase provides robust authentication options and security rules to protect user data.

In the subsequent sections of this book, we will explore each of Firebase's capabilities in more detail, providing practical examples and best practices to help you harness the full potential of this versatile platform. Whether you're building a simple mobile app or a complex web application, Firebase can be a valuable tool in your development toolkit.

1.2 The Evolution of Firebase: From Realtime Database to Full-Stack Development

Firebase has come a long way since its inception, evolving into a full-stack development platform that offers a wide range of services and capabilities. Understanding the evolution of Firebase is essential to grasp the platform's capabilities and how it can address various app development needs.

The Early Days: Realtime Database

Firebase started its journey with the introduction of the Realtime Database. This NoSQL database was built on the concept of synchronization in real-time, making it ideal for applications that required live updates and collaboration features. Developers quickly adopted Firebase for building chat applications, collaborative tools, and multiplayer games.

The Realtime Database uses a JSON-like data structure, which makes it easy to work with for developers familiar with JavaScript. Data changes in the database are immediately pushed to all connected clients, enabling real-time updates without the need for manual polling or refreshing.

```javascript
// Firebase Realtime Database example
const firebaseConfig = {
  apiKey: "YOUR_API_KEY",
  authDomain: "YOUR_AUTH_DOMAIN",
  databaseURL: "YOUR_DATABASE_URL",
  projectId: "YOUR_PROJECT_ID",
  storageBucket: "YOUR_STORAGE_BUCKET",
  messagingSenderId: "YOUR_MESSAGING_SENDER_ID",
  appId: "YOUR_APP_ID"
};

// Initialize Firebase
firebase.initializeApp(firebaseConfig);

// Reference to a specific node in the database
const database = firebase.database();
const messagesRef = database.ref('messages');

// Listen for changes in the database
messagesRef.on('value', (snapshot) => {
  const data = snapshot.val();
  // Update UI with new data
});
```

Expanding Capabilities: Firebase Authentication and Cloud Firestore

As Firebase gained popularity, Google expanded its offerings to cover various aspects of app development. Firebase Authentication was introduced, making it easy for developers to handle user authentication and authorization. It supports various authentication providers, including email/password, Google, Facebook, and more, simplifying the implementation of secure user accounts in apps.

```javascript
// Firebase Authentication example
const auth = firebase.auth();

// Sign up a new user with email and password
auth.createUserWithEmailAndPassword(email, password)
  .then((userCredential) => {
    // User signed up successfully
    const user = userCredential.user;
  })
  .catch((error) => {
    // Handle errors
  });
```

Cloud Firestore was introduced as a more scalable and flexible NoSQL database option, addressing some of the limitations of the Realtime Database. Firestore allows for complex querying, hierarchical data structures, and more robust security rules. It became the preferred choice for many developers building larger and data-intensive applications.

```javascript
// Firebase Firestore example
const firestore = firebase.firestore();

// Add a new document to a collection
firestore.collection("users").add({
  name: "John Doe",
  email: "john@example.com",
  age: 30
})
  .then((docRef) => {
    console.log("Document written with ID: ", docRef.id);
  })
  .catch((error) => {
    console.error("Error adding document: ", error);
  });
```

A Complete Development Platform

Firebase continued to expand its offerings, becoming a comprehensive app development platform. It introduced Firebase Storage for managing user-generated content, Firebase Hosting for web app deployment, Firebase Functions for serverless computing, Firebase Analytics for user insights, and more.

Developers now have the flexibility to choose the Firebase services that best suit their project's requirements, from building a simple mobile app to creating a complex, multi-platform application. Firebase's integration with other Google services and its emphasis on real-time capabilities make it a compelling choice for modern app development.

In the subsequent sections of this book, we will explore each of these Firebase services in detail, providing practical examples and best practices to help you leverage Firebase's full-stack development capabilities effectively.

1.3 Firebase vs. Traditional Backend Solutions

When considering a backend solution for your mobile or web application, you'll often come across the choice between using Firebase or traditional backend solutions. Each approach has its advantages and limitations, and it's crucial to understand the differences before making a decision.

Firebase: A Serverless Approach

Firebase adopts a serverless architecture, which means you don't need to manage your own servers or infrastructure. Firebase takes care of server provisioning, scaling, and maintenance, allowing you to focus solely on your app's front-end development and logic. This serverless approach offers several benefits:

1. **Simplified Development**: With Firebase, you can get started quickly without the need to set up and manage servers. This accelerates the development process, especially for small to medium-sized projects.

2. **Real-time Capabilities**: Firebase is renowned for its real-time synchronization features, making it an excellent choice for applications that require instant updates and collaboration features. Real-time database updates are automatically propagated to all connected clients.

3. **Scalability**: Firebase can automatically scale to handle increased user loads and data demands. You don't need to worry about provisioning additional servers or optimizing for scalability.

4. **Integration with Other Google Services**: Firebase seamlessly integrates with other Google Cloud services, providing access to machine learning, analytics, cloud storage, and more.

5. **Authentication and Security**: Firebase offers robust authentication and security features, including user authentication, access control rules, and encryption, to protect your app and user data.

6. **Cost-Effective**: Firebase's pricing model is often more cost-effective for smaller projects and startups, as you pay based on usage rather than infrastructure maintenance.

```
// Firebase serverless functions example
// This function is triggered when a new user signs up
exports.sendWelcomeEmail = functions.auth.user().onCreate((user) => {
  // Send a welcome email to the new user
});
```

Traditional Backend Solutions

Traditional backend solutions involve setting up and managing your own servers or using cloud-based virtual machines. While this approach offers more control and customization, it comes with some challenges:

1. **Server Management**: You are responsible for server provisioning, maintenance, and scaling. This can be time-consuming and requires expertise in server administration.

2. **Development Time**: Setting up a custom backend can extend the development timeline, especially for complex projects, as you need to implement various server components.

3. **Real-time Features**: Implementing real-time features in a traditional backend can be challenging and may require additional libraries or third-party services.

4. **Scalability**: Scalability depends on your infrastructure setup, and scaling up may require significant effort and cost.

5. **Cost and Complexity**: Traditional backend solutions may involve higher initial costs for server infrastructure and ongoing maintenance expenses.

```
// Traditional server setup example using Node.js and Express.js
const express = require('express');
const app = express();
const port = 3000;

app.get('/', (req, res) => {
  res.send('Hello, World!');
});

app.listen(port, () => {
  console.log(`Server listening at http://localhost:${port}`);
});
```

Choosing the Right Solution

The choice between Firebase and traditional backend solutions depends on your project's specific requirements and constraints. Here are some factors to consider:

- **Project Complexity**: For simple projects or prototypes, Firebase's serverless approach can save time and effort. For complex projects with specific infrastructure needs, traditional solutions may be more suitable.

- **Real-time Features**: If your app heavily relies on real-time features like live chats, collaborative editing, or live sports updates, Firebase's real-time capabilities are a significant advantage.

- **Cost**: Consider your budget and cost projections. Firebase's pricing model may be more favorable for smaller projects, but costs can increase as your user base grows.

- **Control**: Traditional solutions offer more control over your backend infrastructure, which may be essential for specific use cases or compliance requirements.

In summary, Firebase's serverless architecture is a powerful choice for many app development scenarios, particularly when rapid development, real-time features, and scalability are crucial. However, for projects with specific infrastructure needs or complex requirements, traditional backend solutions may offer greater flexibility and control. It's essential to assess your project's unique needs and evaluate both options to make an informed decision.

1.4 Setting Up a Firebase Project

Before you can start using Firebase for your mobile or web application, you need to set up a Firebase project. This involves creating a project in the Firebase Console, configuring your app, and obtaining the necessary credentials. Here's a step-by-step guide to setting up a Firebase project:

Step 1: Create a Firebase Project

1. Visit the Firebase Console.

2. Click on the "Add Project" button to create a new project.

3. Provide a name for your project. This name is for identification purposes and can be changed later if needed.

4. You can also choose to enable Google Analytics for your project during this step. Analytics can provide valuable insights into user behavior and app performance. Click "Continue" when you're ready.

Step 2: Configure Your App

1. After creating the project, you'll be prompted to add an app to your project. Select the platform (iOS, Android, or web) for your app.

2. Provide the necessary details for your app, such as the app's nickname and the platform-specific details (e.g., iOS bundle ID, Android package name). These details ensure that Firebase services are correctly linked to your app.

3. Click "Register app" to add your app to the project.

To use Firebase services in your app, you need to integrate the Firebase SDK. Firebase provides SDKs for various platforms, including iOS, Android, and web.

For iOS:

1. Download the `GoogleService-Info.plist` file from the Firebase Console.

2. Add the `GoogleService-Info.plist` file to your Xcode project.

3. Install the Firebase SDK using CocoaPods or manually by following the instructions provided in the Firebase Console.

For Android:

1. Download the `google-services.json` file from the Firebase Console.

2. Add the `google-services.json` file to your Android app module.

3. Add the Firebase SDK dependencies to your app's build.gradle file.

For Web:

1. In the Firebase Console, go to Project settings and click on the "General" tab.

2. Under the "Your apps" section, find the web app you added earlier and click on the Firebase SDK snippet icon (</>).

3. Copy the Firebase configuration object, which includes your Firebase project's configuration settings.

4. In your web app's code, initialize Firebase with the configuration object.

Step 4: Add Firebase Services

You can choose which Firebase services to enable for your project based on your app's requirements. Firebase offers a wide range of services, including Realtime Database, Firestore, Authentication, Storage, Hosting, Functions, Analytics, and more.

To add a service:

1. In the Firebase Console, navigate to your project.

2. Click on "Build" in the left sidebar.

3. Click on the "Add app" button and select the platform (iOS, Android, or web) you want to add the service to.

4. Follow the on-screen instructions to add the specific service to your app.

If you're using Firebase Authentication, make sure to configure authentication methods and set up security rules for your Firebase project. Security rules control who has access to your Firebase resources and what they can do with them.

Firebase provides a rule simulator to help you test your security rules and ensure they meet your app's requirements while maintaining security.

```
// Example Firebase security rules for Firestore
rules_version = '2';
service cloud.firestore {
  match /databases/{database}/documents {
    // Allow authenticated users to read and write their own data
    match /users/{userId} {
      allow read, write: if request.auth.uid == userId;
    }
  }
}
```

Step 6: Testing and Development

Before deploying your app to production, it's essential to thoroughly test it in a development environment. Firebase provides tools for local testing and debugging, such as the Firebase Emulator Suite, which allows you to test Firebase services locally.

Ensure that your app's integration with Firebase services works as expected and that authentication, data storage, and other functionality are functioning correctly.

Step 7: Deployment and Monitoring

Once you've thoroughly tested your app, you can deploy it to production. Firebase provides hosting for web apps, and you can use various deployment methods for mobile apps, depending on the platform.

Monitor your app's performance and user behavior using Firebase Analytics and Performance Monitoring. Firebase offers real-time insights and crash reporting to help you identify and resolve issues quickly.

Setting up a Firebase project is a crucial step in the development process, and it provides a solid foundation for building and maintaining your mobile or web application. Firebase's user-friendly console and documentation make the setup process relatively straightforward, allowing you to focus on creating a feature-rich and responsive app.

1.5 Overview of Firebase Services and Features

Firebase offers a comprehensive suite of services and features designed to simplify app development, enhance user experiences, and drive app growth. Understanding these services and how they can benefit your project is essential. In this section, we will provide an overview of the key Firebase services and their features.

Realtime Database

The Firebase Realtime Database is a NoSQL cloud-hosted database that allows you to store and sync data in real-time. It is particularly useful for building collaborative applications, chat apps, and any app that requires synchronized data across devices. Key features include real-time synchronization, JSON-like data structure, offline support, and data security rules.

Cloud Firestore

Firestore is Firebase's next-generation NoSQL database. It offers more advanced querying capabilities, hierarchical data modeling, and a richer data structure. Firestore is suitable for larger and more complex applications that require scalability and flexibility. It also provides offline support, real-time updates, and robust security rules.

Firebase Authentication

Firebase Authentication simplifies user authentication and authorization for your app. It supports various authentication methods, including email/password, Google, Facebook, Twitter, and more. You can also implement custom authentication flows and multi-factor authentication. Firebase Authentication ensures secure access to your app's resources.

Firebase Storage

Firebase Storage provides scalable cloud storage for user-generated content such as images, videos, and files. It offers easy integration with other Firebase services and allows you to securely store and retrieve user-generated content. Firebase Storage is suitable for applications that handle media uploads and downloads.

Firebase Hosting

Firebase Hosting allows you to deploy web applications quickly and easily. It supports static and dynamic content, offers SSL support, and can be used for single-page applications (SPAs) and progressive web apps (PWAs). Firebase Hosting simplifies web app deployment and provides global content delivery through Content Delivery Network (CDN) integration.

Firebase Functions

Firebase Functions is a serverless compute platform that enables you to run backend code in response to events. You can use it to execute code triggered by database changes, HTTP requests, or other events. Firebase Functions supports Node.js, Python, Go, and other languages, making it flexible and powerful for serverless architecture.

Analytics with Firebase

Firebase Analytics provides insights into user behavior and app performance. It allows you to track user engagement, monitor key events, and measure the impact of changes. Firebase Analytics integrates seamlessly with other Firebase services, providing a comprehensive view of your app's performance and user interactions.

Firebase Performance Monitoring

Firebase Performance Monitoring helps you analyze and optimize your app's performance. It provides data on app startup times, network latency, and other critical performance metrics. You can identify and resolve performance issues to ensure a smooth user experience.

Firebase Cloud Messaging (FCM)

Firebase Cloud Messaging (FCM) enables you to send messages and notifications to users across different platforms, including Android, iOS, and web. It supports targeted messaging, topic-based messaging, and delivery customization. FCM helps you engage and re-engage users with timely notifications.

Machine Learning with Firebase

Firebase integrates with Google's machine learning services, making it easier to add machine learning capabilities to your app. You can implement features like image recognition, natural language processing, and predictive modeling. Machine learning enhances user experiences and provides data-driven insights.

Firebase Extensions

Firebase Extensions are pre-packaged solutions that automate common development tasks. They allow you to extend Firebase functionality without writing custom code. Extensions cover a wide range of use cases, from sending email notifications to resizing images and more.

Cross-Platform Development with Firebase

Firebase supports cross-platform development, allowing you to build applications for iOS, Android, and web using a single codebase. Firebase tools and libraries simplify cross-platform development, making it easier to maintain and update your app across multiple platforms.

Advanced Topics in Firebase

Firebase offers advanced features for custom backend services, integration with machine learning and AI, complex queries and data aggregation, geo-distribution, and multi-region setup. These advanced topics empower you to create sophisticated and high-performance applications.

The final chapter of this book guides you through the process of planning, designing, and building a complete Firebase application. It covers frontend integration, user experience design, testing, deployment, and monitoring, providing a holistic approach to app development.

Firebase's extensive range of services and features caters to a wide variety of app development needs. As you explore each service in detail throughout this book, you'll gain the knowledge and skills to leverage Firebase effectively in your projects, from simple mobile apps to complex multi-platform applications.

Chapter 2: Firebase Authentication

2.1 Introduction to User Authentication

User authentication is a fundamental aspect of many mobile and web applications. It involves verifying the identity of users and allowing them to access specific resources and features within an app. Firebase Authentication provides a robust and easy-to-use solution for implementing user authentication in your Firebase-powered applications.

The Importance of User Authentication

User authentication serves several critical purposes in an application:

1. **Security**: Authentication ensures that only authorized users can access sensitive data or perform specific actions within the app. It protects user data and prevents unauthorized access.

2. **Personalization**: Authentication allows apps to provide a personalized experience for users. It enables features like user profiles, saved preferences, and content recommendations.

3. **Data Ownership**: Authenticated users can have ownership of their data and contributions within the app. This ownership is essential for collaborative platforms, social networks, and e-commerce sites.

4. **Access Control**: Authentication determines who can access particular sections of an app or perform specific actions. It enables role-based access control, ensuring that users have appropriate permissions.

Firebase Authentication Features

Firebase Authentication offers a wide range of features and authentication methods:

Email and Password Authentication

Firebase allows users to sign up and log in using their email and password. It includes features like email verification and password reset.

```
// Firebase email and password authentication example
const auth = firebase.auth();

// Sign up a new user
auth.createUserWithEmailAndPassword(email, password)
  .then((userCredential) => {
    // User signed up successfully
    const user = userCredential.user;
  })
  .catch((error) => {
```

```javascript
      // Handle errors
   });
```


Social Authentication

Firebase supports social authentication providers such as Google, Facebook, Twitter, GitHub, and more. This enables users to log in using their existing social media accounts.

```javascript
// Firebase social authentication example (Google)
const provider = new firebase.auth.GoogleAuthProvider();

// Sign in with Google
auth.signInWithPopup(provider)
  .then((userCredential) => {
    // User signed in successfully
    const user = userCredential.user;
  })
  .catch((error) => {
    // Handle errors
  });
```

Multi-Factor Authentication (MFA)

Firebase allows you to implement multi-factor authentication for added security. Users can verify their identity using methods like SMS, email, or authenticator apps.

Anonymous Authentication

Anonymous authentication enables users to access the app without creating an account. Later, they can choose to upgrade to a full account.

```javascript
// Firebase anonymous authentication example
auth.signInAnonymously()
  .then((userCredential) => {
    // User signed in anonymously
    const user = userCredential.user;
  })
  .catch((error) => {
    // Handle errors
  });
```

Custom Authentication

For unique authentication flows or integration with existing systems, Firebase allows you to implement custom authentication.

```javascript
// Firebase custom authentication example
// Implement your custom authentication logic
```

Firebase Authentication Benefits

Firebase Authentication offers several advantages for developers:

- **Ease of Integration**: Firebase Authentication is easy to set up and integrates seamlessly with other Firebase services.

- **Built-In Security**: Firebase handles authentication securely, including password storage and protection against common attacks like account enumeration.

- **Authentication State**: Firebase provides real-time authentication state monitoring, allowing you to respond to login and logout events in your app.

- **Authentication Providers**: You can choose from a variety of authentication providers, making it convenient for users to log in using their preferred methods.

- **Scalability**: Firebase Authentication scales effortlessly as your app grows, handling user authentication at any scale.

In the subsequent sections of this chapter, we will delve into each authentication method in more detail, providing implementation examples and best practices to ensure a secure and user-friendly authentication process in your Firebase-powered applications.

2.2 Implementing Email and Password Authentication

Email and password authentication is one of the most common and straightforward methods for user authentication in Firebase. It allows users to create an account using their email addresses and set a password for authentication. In this section, we'll explore how to implement email and password authentication in your Firebase-powered application.

Setting Up Firebase Email and Password Authentication

Before you can implement email and password authentication, you need to set up Firebase Authentication in your Firebase project. Follow these steps:

1. In the Firebase Console, navigate to your project.

2. Click on "Authentication" in the left sidebar.

3. Go to the "Sign-in method" tab.

4. Enable "Email/Password" as a sign-in provider.

User Registration

To allow users to register with their email and password, you can create a registration form in your app. Here's a simplified example using HTML and JavaScript:

```html
<!-- HTML Registration Form -->
<form id="registration-form">
  <label for="email">Email:</label>
```

```html
  <input type="email" id="email" required>
  <br>
  <label for="password">Password:</label>
  <input type="password" id="password" required>
  <br>
  <button type="submit">Register</button>
</form>
```

```javascript
// JavaScript for User Registration
const auth = firebase.auth();

document.getElementById('registration-form').addEventListener('submit', (e) => {
  e.preventDefault();
  const email = document.getElementById('email').value;
  const password = document.getElementById('password').value;

  auth.createUserWithEmailAndPassword(email, password)
    .then((userCredential) => {
      // User registered successfully
      const user = userCredential.user;
      console.log('User registered:', user.email);
    })
    .catch((error) => {
      // Handle registration errors
      console.error('Registration failed:', error.message);
    });
});
```

In this code, we first create an HTML form where users can enter their email and password. When the form is submitted, we use the `createUserWithEmailAndPassword` method provided by Firebase Authentication to register the user. If successful, we can access the registered user's information.

User Login

Implementing user login with email and password is similar to registration. Here's a basic example:

```html
<!-- HTML Login Form -->
<form id="login-form">
  <label for="login-email">Email:</label>
  <input type="email" id="login-email" required>
  <br>
  <label for="login-password">Password:</label>
  <input type="password" id="login-password" required>
  <br>
  <button type="submit">Login</button>
</form>
```

```javascript
// JavaScript for User Login
document.getElementById('login-form').addEventListener('submit', (e) => {
  e.preventDefault();
  const loginEmail = document.getElementById('login-email').value;
  const loginPassword = document.getElementById('login-password').value;

  auth.signInWithEmailAndPassword(loginEmail, loginPassword)
    .then((userCredential) => {
      // User logged in successfully
      const user = userCredential.user;
      console.log('User logged in:', user.email);
    })
    .catch((error) => {
      // Handle login errors
      console.error('Login failed:', error.message);
    });
});
```

In this code, we create another HTML form for user login. When the form is submitted, we use the `signInWithEmailAndPassword` method to authenticate the user. If the login is successful, we can access the user's information.

Password Reset

Firebase also provides a convenient way to allow users to reset their passwords if they forget them. Here's an example of how to implement password reset:

```html
<!-- HTML Password Reset Form -->
<form id="password-reset-form">
  <label for="reset-email">Email:</label>
  <input type="email" id="reset-email" required>
  <br>
  <button type="submit">Reset Password</button>
</form>
```

```javascript
// JavaScript for Password Reset
document.getElementById('password-reset-form').addEventListener('submit', (e) => {
  e.preventDefault();
  const resetEmail = document.getElementById('reset-email').value;

  auth.sendPasswordResetEmail(resetEmail)
    .then(() => {
      // Password reset email sent successfully
      console.log('Password reset email sent to:', resetEmail);
    })
    .catch((error) => {
      // Handle password reset errors
      console.error('Password reset failed:', error.message);
```

```
    });
});
```

In this code, users can enter their email address, and when they submit the form, Firebase's `sendPasswordResetEmail` method sends them an email with instructions to reset their password.

Security Considerations

When implementing email and password authentication, it's essential to consider security:

- **Password Storage**: Firebase securely stores passwords using salted and hashed algorithms, ensuring that passwords are not stored in plaintext.

- **User Data**: Be cautious about the data you collect from users during registration. Only collect necessary information and ensure that sensitive data is stored securely.

- **Authentication State**: Always monitor the authentication state in your app to control access to sensitive features or data.

- **Rate Limiting**: Implement rate limiting and account lockout mechanisms to protect against brute force attacks.

Implementing email and password authentication with Firebase is a reliable and secure way to handle user registration and login in your applications. Firebase Authentication simplifies the process, allowing you to focus on building features and providing a seamless user experience.

2.3 Social Authentication: Google, Facebook, and Others

Social authentication is a popular and convenient way to allow users to log in to your app using their existing social media accounts. Firebase Authentication supports various social authentication providers, including Google, Facebook, Twitter, GitHub, and more. In this section, we will explore how to implement social authentication in your Firebase-powered application.

Setting Up Social Authentication Providers

Before implementing social authentication, you need to configure the respective social providers in your Firebase project. Here's how to set up some of the commonly used providers:

Google Authentication

1. Go to the Google Cloud Console.

2. Create a new project or select an existing one.

3. In the left sidebar, click on "APIs & Services" and then "Credentials."

4. Click on the "Create credentials" button and select "OAuth client ID."

5. Choose "Web application" as the application type.

6. Enter the authorized JavaScript origins and redirect URIs for your Firebase project. You can find these in the Firebase Console under "Authentication" > "Sign-in method" > "Google."

7. Click "Create" to generate your OAuth client ID.

8. Copy the generated client ID.

9. In the Firebase Console, navigate to your project and go to "Authentication" > "Sign-in method" > "Google." Enable the provider and paste the client ID in the respective field.

Facebook Authentication

1. Go to the Facebook Developers website.

2. Create a new app or select an existing one.

3. In the app dashboard, go to "Settings" > "Basic."

4. Note down the "App ID" and "App Secret."

5. In the Firebase Console, navigate to your project and go to "Authentication" > "Sign-in method" > "Facebook." Enable the provider and enter the "App ID" and "App Secret."

Twitter Authentication

1. Go to the Twitter Developer website.

2. Create a Twitter Developer account and create a new Twitter app.

3. Note down the "API Key" and "API Secret Key."

4. In the Firebase Console, navigate to your project and go to "Authentication" > "Sign-in method" > "Twitter." Enable the provider and enter the "API Key" and "API Secret Key."

GitHub Authentication

1. Go to the GitHub Developer website.

2. Create a new OAuth App in your GitHub account settings.

3. Note down the "Client ID" and "Client Secret."

4. In the Firebase Console, navigate to your project and go to "Authentication" > "Sign-in method" > "GitHub." Enable the provider and enter the "Client ID" and "Client Secret."

Once you have set up the social authentication providers in your Firebase project, you can implement social login in your app.

Google Authentication

Here's an example of how to implement Google authentication using Firebase in a web app:

```javascript
// Initialize Firebase
const firebaseConfig = {
  apiKey: "YOUR_API_KEY",
  authDomain: "YOUR_AUTH_DOMAIN",
  projectId: "YOUR_PROJECT_ID",
  storageBucket: "YOUR_STORAGE_BUCKET",
  messagingSenderId: "YOUR_MESSAGING_SENDER_ID",
  appId: "YOUR_APP_ID"
};


firebase.initializeApp(firebaseConfig);


// Google Sign-In
const auth = firebase.auth();
const provider = new firebase.auth.GoogleAuthProvider();


document.getElementById('google-sign-in').addEventListener('click', () => {
  auth.signInWithPopup(provider)
    .then((userCredential) => {
      // User signed in with Google
      const user = userCredential.user;
      console.log('User signed in with Google:', user.displayName);
    })
    .catch((error) => {
      // Handle Google sign-in errors
      console.error('Google sign-in failed:', error.message);
    });
});
```

In this code, we first initialize Firebase with your project's configuration. We then create an instance of the Google authentication provider and attach it to a button click event. When the user clicks the button, they can sign in with their Google account using the Firebase `signInWithPopup` method.

Here's an example of how to implement Facebook authentication using Firebase in a web app:

```javascript
// Facebook Sign-In
const facebookProvider = new firebase.auth.FacebookAuthProvider();

document.getElementById('facebook-sign-in').addEventListener('click', () => {
  auth.signInWithPopup(facebookProvider)
    .then((userCredential) => {
      // User signed in with Facebook
      const user = userCredential.user;
      console.log('User signed in with Facebook:', user.displayName);
    })
    .catch((error) => {
      // Handle Facebook sign-in errors
      console.error('Facebook sign-in failed:', error.message);
    });
});
```

In this code, we create an instance of the Facebook authentication provider and attach it to a button click event. Users can sign in with their Facebook accounts using the Firebase signInWithPopup method.

Implementing Twitter authentication using Firebase in a web app:

```javascript
// Twitter Sign-In
const twitterProvider = new firebase.auth.TwitterAuthProvider();

document.getElementById('twitter-sign-in').addEventListener('click', () => {
  auth.signInWithPopup(twitterProvider)
    .then((userCredential) => {
      // User signed in with Twitter
      const user = userCredential.user;
      console.log('User signed in with Twitter:', user.displayName);
    })
    .catch((error) => {
      // Handle Twitter sign-in errors
      console.error('Twitter sign-in failed:', error.message);
    });
});
```

In this code, we create an instance of the Twitter authentication provider and attach it to a button click event. Users can sign in with their Twitter accounts using the Firebase signInWithPopup method.

Implementing GitHub authentication using Firebase in a web app:

```javascript
// GitHub Sign-In
const githubProvider = new firebase.auth.GithubAuthProvider();

document.getElementById('github-sign-in').addEventListener('click', () => {
  auth.signInWithPopup(githubProvider)
    .then((userCredential) => {
      // User signed in with GitHub
      const user = userCredential.user;
      console.log('User signed in with GitHub:', user.displayName);
    })
    .catch((error) => {
      // Handle GitHub sign-in errors
      console.error('GitHub sign-in failed:', error.message);
    });
});
```

In this code, we create an instance of the GitHub authentication provider and attach it to a button click event. Users can sign in with their GitHub accounts using the Firebase signInWithPopup method.

Security Considerations

2.4 Advanced Features: Anonymous and Multi-Factor Authentication

Firebase Authentication offers advanced features that enhance security and user experience in your app. In this section, we'll explore two of these features: Anonymous Authentication and Multi-Factor Authentication (MFA).

Anonymous Authentication

Anonymous authentication allows users to access your app without requiring them to create an account or sign in with their credentials. Firebase assigns a unique anonymous identifier to each user, which can be converted to a full account later if the user chooses to do so. This feature is particularly useful when you want to provide a frictionless experience for users who may want to explore your app before committing to full registration.

Here's how to implement anonymous authentication in Firebase:

```javascript
// Anonymous Sign-In
auth.signInAnonymously()
  .then((userCredential) => {
    // User signed in anonymously
    const user = userCredential.user;
    console.log('User signed in anonymously:', user.uid);
```

```javascript
  })
  .catch((error) => {
    // Handle anonymous sign-in errors
    console.error('Anonymous sign-in failed:', error.message);
  });
```

In this code, when the user chooses anonymous sign-in, Firebase generates an anonymous user account, and you can access the unique user identifier (UID) to associate data or actions with this anonymous user.

Multi-Factor Authentication (MFA)

Multi-Factor Authentication (MFA) is a crucial security feature that adds an extra layer of protection to user accounts by requiring them to provide two or more authentication factors. These factors can include something the user knows (e.g., password), something the user has (e.g., a mobile device), or something the user is (e.g., a fingerprint).

Firebase Authentication supports MFA through various methods, including SMS, email, and authenticator apps. Here's an example of enabling SMS-based MFA:

```javascript
// Enabling SMS-based MFA for a user
const user = auth.currentUser;

const phoneNumber = '+1234567890'; // Replace with the user's phone number

const phoneAuth = new firebase.auth.PhoneAuthProvider();

phoneAuth.verifyPhoneNumber(phoneNumber, recaptcha)
  .then((verificationId) => {
    // Verification code sent to the user's phone
    const code = prompt('Enter the verification code sent to your phone:');

    const credential = firebase.auth.PhoneAuthProvider.credential(verificationId, code);

    return user.linkWithCredential(credential);
  })
  .then((userCredential) => {
    // MFA enabled successfully
    const user = userCredential.user;
    console.log('MFA enabled for user:', user.displayName);
  })
  .catch((error) => {
    // Handle MFA setup errors
    console.error('MFA setup failed:', error.message);
  });
```

In this code, we use SMS-based MFA to enable a second layer of authentication. After entering the verification code sent to their phone, the user's account is linked with the MFA method. Subsequently, they will need to provide this second factor during login.

When implementing advanced authentication features like Anonymous Authentication and Multi-Factor Authentication, consider the following security aspects:

- **Data Protection**: Ensure that even anonymous users have limited access to sensitive data and actions. Always enforce appropriate access controls.

- **MFA Recovery**: Provide a secure way for users to recover their accounts if they lose access to their MFA methods, such as backup codes or alternate contact methods.

- **User Experience**: Balancing security with a seamless user experience is crucial. MFA should enhance security without causing user frustration.

- **Monitoring and Reporting**: Implement monitoring and reporting for MFA events to detect any unusual activity or security breaches.

These advanced authentication features in Firebase provide powerful tools to protect user accounts and offer flexible options for different use cases. Integrating these features appropriately into your app can enhance security and user satisfaction.

2.5 Best Practices for Secure Authentication

When implementing authentication in your Firebase-powered application, it's crucial to prioritize security to protect user data and maintain trust. In this section, we'll explore best practices for secure authentication.

1. Use Strong Password Policies

Enforce strong password policies to ensure that users create secure passwords. Require a minimum length, a combination of upper and lower case letters, numbers, and special characters. Firebase Authentication provides customizable password complexity settings to help you achieve this.

2. Implement Rate Limiting

Implement rate limiting for authentication requests to protect against brute force attacks. Firebase offers security rules and configurations to limit the number of authentication attempts within a specific time frame.

3. Enable Multi-Factor Authentication (MFA)

Encourage users to enable MFA for their accounts. MFA adds an extra layer of security by requiring users to provide multiple authentication factors. Firebase supports various MFA methods, including SMS, email, and authenticator apps.

4. Monitor Authentication Events

Set up monitoring and alerting for authentication events. Regularly review logs and reports for suspicious activity. Firebase provides real-time event monitoring and integration with Firebase Analytics for tracking user behavior.

5. Use Secure Connection (HTTPS)

Ensure that your app communicates with Firebase Authentication over a secure HTTPS connection. This prevents data interception during authentication.

6. Validate User Input

Always validate and sanitize user input to prevent security vulnerabilities such as SQL injection or cross-site scripting (XSS) attacks. Firebase provides security rules for controlling data access and validation.

7. Securely Store User Data

Protect user data by adhering to Firebase security rules. Define rules that limit access to sensitive user information to authorized users only.

8. Handle Password Resets Securely

Implement secure password reset mechanisms. Firebase's `sendPasswordResetEmail` function securely sends password reset instructions to the user's registered email address.

9. Educate Users on Security

Educate your users about security best practices. Provide guidance on creating strong passwords, enabling MFA, and recognizing phishing attempts.

10. Keep Firebase SDKs Up to Date

Regularly update Firebase SDKs to the latest versions. Firebase continually releases updates that include security enhancements and bug fixes.

11. Secure API Keys and Secrets

Protect API keys and secrets used in your Firebase project. Avoid hardcoding these credentials in your app's source code and use environment variables or a secure storage solution.

12. Plan for Account Recovery

Implement a secure account recovery process for users who lose access to their accounts. Offer options like email-based account recovery or backup codes for MFA.

13. Implement Cross-Origin Resource Sharing (CORS)

If your app uses Firebase Authentication for web applications, configure Cross-Origin Resource Sharing (CORS) settings to restrict access to only trusted domains.

14. Regularly Review Security Best Practices

Stay informed about the latest security best practices and vulnerabilities. Regularly review and update your app's security measures to address emerging threats.

15. Conduct Security Audits

Periodically conduct security audits and penetration testing to identify and address potential vulnerabilities in your authentication system.

By following these best practices, you can enhance the security of your Firebase Authentication implementation and provide a safer environment for your users. Security should be an ongoing consideration throughout the development and maintenance of your app.

Chapter 3: Realtime Database

3.1 Understanding Realtime Database

Firebase Realtime Database is a NoSQL, cloud-hosted database that allows you to store and synchronize data in real-time between clients. It's a part of Firebase's suite of products, designed to help you build feature-rich applications quickly and efficiently. In this section, we will delve into the core concepts and features of the Realtime Database.

Key Concepts

JSON Data Structure

The Firebase Realtime Database stores data in a JSON-like tree structure. Each piece of data is represented as a key-value pair, where keys are strings and values can be various types: strings, numbers, booleans, objects, or even other nested JSON-like structures.

```json
{
  "users": {
    "user1": {
      "name": "Alice",
      "email": "alice@example.com"
    },
    "user2": {
      "name": "Bob",
      "email": "bob@example.com"
    }
  }
}
```

In this example, the "users" node contains two user objects, each with a unique identifier ("user1" and "user2").

Real-Time Data Synchronization

One of the key features of the Realtime Database is its ability to synchronize data across multiple clients in real-time. When data changes on the server, all connected clients are notified and receive the updated data immediately. This enables real-time collaboration and ensures that all clients have consistent data.

Offline Data Access

Firebase Realtime Database provides built-in support for offline data access. Clients can read and write data even when they are not connected to the internet. Any changes made offline are synchronized with the server once the connection is reestablished.

The data in the Realtime Database is organized into a hierarchical structure, similar to a file system. The top-level node is referred to as the root, and you can create child nodes beneath it to structure your data as needed.

For example:

```
/
  |-- users
  |     |-- user1
  |     |     |-- name: "Alice"
  |     |     |-- email: "alice@example.com"
  |     |
  |     |-- user2
  |     |     |-- name: "Bob"
  |     |     |-- email: "bob@example.com"
  |
  |-- posts
        |-- post1
        |     |-- title: "Introduction to Firebase"
        |     |-- content: "Firebase is a powerful..."
        |
        |-- post2
              |-- title: "Realtime Data Synchronization"
              |-- content: "Firebase Realtime Database..."
```

In this example, there are two top-level nodes: "users" and "posts," each containing child nodes with data.

Event-Driven Programming Model

To interact with the Realtime Database, you use an event-driven programming model. Clients can attach listeners to specific nodes or queries, and these listeners are triggered whenever data at that location changes. Common events include "value" (when data changes) and "child_added," "child_changed," and "child_removed" (when child nodes change).

Here's an example in JavaScript of attaching a "value" event listener to retrieve user data:

```javascript
const database = firebase.database();
const userRef = database.ref('users/user1');

userRef.on('value', (snapshot) => {
  const userData = snapshot.val();
  console.log('User data:', userData);
});
```

In this code, the "value" event listener is set up to fetch user data whenever it changes.

Firebase Realtime Database provides a powerful security rules system that allows you to control who has access to your data and what actions they can perform. Security rules are defined using a custom language and can enforce authentication, data validation, and fine-grained access control.

For example, you can restrict access to the "users" node to authenticated users only:

```
{
  "rules": {
    ".read": "auth != null",
    ".write": "auth != null",
    "users": {
      "$user_id": {
        ".read": "$user_id === auth.uid",
        ".write": "$user_id === auth.uid"
      }
    }
  }
}
```

In this rule set, users can only read and write data under the "users" node if they are authenticated, and they can only access their own data based on their user ID.

Use Cases

Firebase Realtime Database is suitable for a wide range of use cases, including:

- **Real-time Collaboration**: Build real-time collaborative apps like chat applications, collaborative document editing, and live multiplayer games.

- **User Data**: Store user profiles, preferences, and data in a structured manner.

- **Content Management**: Manage dynamic content such as blog posts, comments, and product listings.

- **IoT and Sensor Data**: Collect and analyze data from Internet of Things (IoT) devices and sensors in real-time.

- **Live Updates**: Provide live updates for news feeds, sports scores, and social media timelines.

Limitations

While Firebase Realtime Database is powerful and flexible, it has some limitations to be aware of:

- **Limited Querying

3.2 Structuring and Managing Data

Structuring and managing data effectively is essential when working with Firebase Realtime Database. Proper organization and data modeling can significantly impact the performance and scalability of your application. In this section, we'll explore best practices for structuring and managing data in the Realtime Database.

Hierarchical Structure

The Realtime Database uses a hierarchical structure, similar to a JSON tree. To create a well-organized database, consider the following guidelines:

- **Use Nodes for Categories**: Organize your data into nodes that represent categories or entities in your application. For example, in an e-commerce app, you might have nodes for "products," "users," and "orders."

- **Avoid Deep Nesting**: While nesting data is common, avoid excessive nesting (deep hierarchies) as it can make queries and updates complex. Strive for a balance between nesting and flat structures.

```
// Example of a balanced structure
{
  "products": {
    "product1": { /* ... */ },
    "product2": { /* ... */ }
  },
  "users": {
    "user1": { /* ... */ },
    "user2": { /* ... */ }
  },
  "orders": {
    "order1": { /* ... */ },
    "order2": { /* ... */ }
  }
}
```

Denormalization

Firebase encourages denormalization, which means duplicating data when necessary to optimize read operations. This is particularly important for real-time applications where minimizing the number of read operations is crucial.

For example, if you have an e-commerce app, you might store product details both under the "products" node and within each user's "orders" to avoid frequent reads of product data when displaying order history.

```
// Storing product details within each user's order
{
```

```json
"users": {
  "user1": {
    "orders": {
      "order1": {
        "product": {
          "productId": "product1",
          "name": "Product A",
          "price": 19.99
        },
        // ...
      },
      // ...
    }
  },
  // ...
}
```

Indexing

Firebase Realtime Database automatically indexes data to make queries efficient. However, you should be aware of Firebase's indexing limitations:

- Indexes are created on a per-path basis.
- Indexes are limited to deep queries (queries with multiple children).
- Compound indexes (queries with multiple criteria) require explicit configuration.

Be mindful of these limitations when designing your data structure and queries.

Security Rules

Security rules play a critical role in data management. They determine who can read and write data and enforce data validation. When designing your rules:

- **Implement Authentication**: Ensure that only authenticated users can access sensitive data. Use `auth != null` in your rules to require authentication.

- **Fine-Grained Access Control**: Use variables like $uid to create fine-grained rules. For example, you can allow users to write to their own data using `"user": { "$uid": { ".write": "$uid === auth.uid" } }`.

- **Data Validation**: Enforce data validation rules to prevent invalid or malicious data from being written to the database.

Monitoring and Scaling

As your application grows, monitoring and scaling become important:

- **Firebase Analytics**: Use Firebase Analytics to gain insights into how users interact with your data. Monitor performance and user behavior to make informed decisions.

- **Scaling**: Firebase automatically handles scaling for you. However, keep an eye on the usage and be ready to adjust your Firebase plan as needed.

- **Backup and Restore**: Regularly back up your data to prevent data loss. Firebase provides tools for exporting and importing data.

- **Offline Access**: Firebase offers offline data access, allowing users to interact with your app even when offline. Ensure your app gracefully handles offline scenarios.

Data Migration

Data schema changes are common during the development lifecycle. Firebase provides tools and techniques for data migration:

- **Atomic Writes**: Use Firebase's multi-location updates to ensure that updates to multiple locations in the database are atomic. This helps maintain data consistency during migrations.

- **Cloud Functions**: Implement data migration using Firebase Cloud Functions. You can automate data transformations and updates in response to specific triggers or changes.

By following these best practices, you can effectively structure and manage data in Firebase Realtime Database, ensuring optimal performance, scalability, and data integrity for your application.

3.3 Realtime Data Synchronization

Realtime data synchronization is one of the core features that sets Firebase Realtime Database apart. It enables multiple clients to stay up-to-date with changes in the data in real-time. In this section, we'll explore how real-time data synchronization works and how to use it effectively in your Firebase-powered applications.

How Real-Time Synchronization Works

Firebase uses WebSocket connections to maintain a persistent connection between the client and the server. When data changes on the server, it immediately pushes those changes to all connected clients. This mechanism ensures that all clients have the most current data, and updates are reflected in real-time.

Here's how the real-time synchronization process typically works:

1. A client initiates a connection to the Firebase Realtime Database.

2. Once connected, the client can listen to specific data locations by adding event listeners. Common events include "value," "child_added," "child_changed," and "child_removed."

3. When changes occur at the specified location, Firebase notifies all clients that are listening to that location, triggering the associated event listener.

4. The event listener receives the updated data, allowing the client to react accordingly, such as updating the user interface.

This real-time synchronization is efficient and minimizes the need for constant polling or manual refreshes by clients.

Implementing Real-Time Synchronization

To implement real-time synchronization in your Firebase application, follow these steps:

1. Initialize Firebase and get a reference to the Realtime Database:

```javascript
const firebaseConfig = {
  apiKey: 'YOUR_API_KEY',
  authDomain: 'YOUR_AUTH_DOMAIN',
  databaseURL: 'YOUR_DATABASE_URL',
  projectId: 'YOUR_PROJECT_ID',
  storageBucket: 'YOUR_STORAGE_BUCKET',
  messagingSenderId: 'YOUR_MESSAGING_SENDER_ID',
  appId: 'YOUR_APP_ID'
};

firebase.initializeApp(firebaseConfig);
const database = firebase.database();
```

2. Add event listeners to specific data locations:

```javascript
const userRef = database.ref('users/user1');

// Listen for changes to user1's data
userRef.on('value', (snapshot) => {
  const userData = snapshot.val();
  console.log('User data:', userData);
});
```

In this example, the "value" event listener is added to the "user1" node. Whenever data changes within this node, the listener is triggered, and the updated data is retrieved.

3. Update data as needed:

```javascript
// Update user1's name
userRef.child('name').set('Updated Name');
```

Changes made to data using the set() method or other update methods are automatically synchronized with connected clients in real-time.

Real-time synchronization is valuable for various use cases, including:

- **Chat Applications**: Displaying real-time messages and updates in chat apps.

- **Collaborative Editing**: Allowing multiple users to collaboratively edit documents or spreadsheets.

- **Live Dashboards**: Displaying live data, such as analytics or monitoring metrics.

- **Multiplayer Games**: Keeping all players in sync with game state changes.

- **Live Notifications**: Providing immediate notifications for events or updates.

Offline Data Access

Firebase Realtime Database also supports offline data access. When a client loses its internet connection, it can continue to read and write data locally. Once the connection is reestablished, Firebase automatically synchronizes the local changes with the server. This ensures a seamless user experience even in offline scenarios.

To enable offline data access, Firebase automatically caches data locally. You don't need to write additional code to implement this feature.

Security Considerations

When using real-time synchronization, consider the security of your data:

- Define appropriate security rules to control who can access and modify data.

- Ensure that sensitive data is not exposed to unauthorized users.

- Avoid exposing Firebase database credentials or API keys in your client-side code.

By leveraging real-time data synchronization, you can create dynamic and interactive applications that keep users engaged and informed with up-to-the-second data updates.

3.4 Securing Your Database with Rules

Securing your Firebase Realtime Database is paramount to protect user data and maintain the integrity of your application. Firebase provides a robust security rules system that allows you to define who has access to your data and what operations they can perform. In this section, we'll explore how to secure your database using security rules effectively.

Firebase Realtime Database security rules are a set of conditions that determine who can read or write data at various database locations. They serve as a barrier between your data and unauthorized users, ensuring that only authenticated users with the appropriate permissions can access specific data.

Security rules are defined using a custom JSON-like language designed specifically for Firebase. These rules are evaluated in real-time when a client tries to read or write data, and access is granted or denied accordingly.

Defining Security Rules

Here's an example of a basic security rule set for a Firebase Realtime Database:

```
{
  "rules": {
    ".read": "auth != null",
    ".write": "auth != null",
    "posts": {
      ".read": "auth != null",
      ".write": "auth != null",
      "$post_id": {
        ".validate": "newData.child('author').val() === auth.uid",
        ".read": "auth != null",
        ".write": "auth != null && data.child('author').val() === auth.uid"
      }
    }
  }
}
```

In this example:

- The top-level rules ensure that only authenticated users can read and write data.

- Under the "posts" node, only authenticated users can read and write data.

- Within each post, the `.validate` rule enforces that the author of the post matches the authenticated user.

- The `.read` and `.write` rules for individual posts check if the user is authenticated and if they are the author of the post.

These rules create a secure environment where only the post's author can modify their posts, and all other users can read the data.

Key Security Rules Concepts

To effectively secure your Firebase Realtime Database, it's important to understand key security rules concepts:

- **auth Object**: The `auth` object represents the authenticated user. You can use it in rules to check if a user is authenticated and access their unique user ID (`auth.uid`).

- **Wildcard Rules ($variable)**: You can use wildcard rules to create dynamic rules based on data values. For example, in the above rules, $post_id represents a wildcard that matches any post ID.

- **`.read` and `.write` Rules**: These rules define who can read and write data at a specific location. Use them to control access at different levels of your database hierarchy.

- **`.validate` Rule**: The `.validate` rule allows you to specify conditions that data must meet to be written to the database. This is useful for enforcing data validation rules.

Here are some best practices for designing security rules:

1. **Implement Authentication**: Require authentication for any data that should only be accessible to authenticated users.

2. **Use Wildcards Wisely**: Use wildcard rules carefully to ensure that they don't grant unintended access.

3. **Keep Rules Simple**: Avoid overly complex rules that are difficult to maintain and verify.

4. **Test Rules Thoroughly**: Firebase provides tools for simulating rule evaluation to test your rules thoroughly before deploying them to production.

5. **Audit and Monitor**: Regularly audit and monitor your security rules to ensure they continue to meet your application's requirements.

6. **Backup Rules**: Keep backups of your security rules to restore them in case of accidental misconfiguration.

7. **Stay Informed**: Stay informed about Firebase updates and security best practices to keep your rules up-to-date.

By following these best practices and carefully crafting your security rules, you can maintain a high level of security for your Firebase Realtime Database and protect your application and user data from unauthorized access and data breaches.

3.5 Common Use Cases and Patterns

Firebase Realtime Database is a versatile tool that can be used to address a wide range of use cases in your application. In this section, we'll explore common use cases and data modeling patterns that can help you effectively structure your data and leverage the power of Firebase Realtime Database.

1. User Profiles

Storing user profiles is a common use case. You can create a "users" node where each user has a unique identifier (usually their authentication UID). Within each user's node, store user-specific information like name, email, profile picture URL, and other relevant details.

Here's an example structure for user profiles:

```
{
  "users": {
    "user1_uid": {
      "name": "Alice",
      "email": "alice@example.com",
      "profilePicUrl": "https://example.com/alice.jpg",
      // Additional user-specific data
    },
    "user2_uid": {
      "name": "Bob",
      "email": "bob@example.com",
      "profilePicUrl": "https://example.com/bob.jpg",
      // Additional user-specific data
    }
  }
}
```

2. Real-Time Chat

Implementing real-time chat applications is another popular use case for Firebase Realtime Database. Create a "messages" node where each message has a unique identifier. Messages can be organized by chat rooms or conversations, with each chat room having its unique identifier.

Here's a simplified structure for a chat application:

```
{
  "chatRooms": {
    "room1_id": {
      "messages": {
        "message1_id": {
          "text": "Hello, world!",
          "sender": "user1_uid",
          "timestamp": 1643587200000
        },
        // Additional messages
```

```
      }
    },
    "room2_id": {
      "messages": {
        // Messages for room 2
      }
    }
  }
}
```

3. Social Media Feeds

Building social media feeds where users can post content and see updates from others is a common use case. Create a "posts" node where each post has a unique identifier. Posts can be sorted by timestamp for chronological ordering.

Here's a simplified structure for social media posts:

```
{
  "posts": {
    "post1_id": {
      "text": "Just posted a photo from my vacation!",
      "author": "user1_uid",
      "timestamp": 1643587200000,
      // Additional post data
    },
    "post2_id": {
      // Details for post 2
    }
  }
}
```

4. Notifications

Managing notifications is crucial in many applications. You can create a "notifications" node to store notification data. Each notification can include information about the sender, the recipient, the notification type, and a timestamp.

Here's a basic structure for notifications:

```
{
  "notifications": {
    "notification1_id": {
      "sender": "user2_uid",
      "recipient": "user1_uid",
      "type": "like",
      "timestamp": 1643587200000,
      // Additional notification data
    },
    "notification2_id": {
      // Details for notification 2
```

```
      }
    }
}
```


Enabling real-time collaboration features like collaborative document editing or whiteboarding requires real-time synchronization of data. You can structure your data to represent collaborative documents or boards, where changes made by one user are immediately reflected for others.

Here's a simplified structure for a collaborative document:

```
{
   "documents": {
     "document1_id": {
       "content": "This is a collaborative document.",
       "lastModifiedBy": "user1_uid",
       "timestamp": 1643587200000,
       // Additional document data
     },
     "document2_id": {
       // Details for document 2
     }
   }
}
```

These are just a few examples of common use cases for Firebase Realtime Database. Depending on your application's requirements, you can adapt and expand these patterns to suit your needs. Firebase's real-time capabilities and flexible data modeling make it a powerful tool for building dynamic and interactive applications.

Chapter 4: Firebase Cloud Firestore

4.1 Introduction to Firestore

Firebase Cloud Firestore is a NoSQL document database that offers seamless integration with Firebase services and real-time data synchronization capabilities. It is designed to store, query, and manage data in a flexible and scalable way for web and mobile applications. In this section, we'll introduce you to Firestore and its key features.

What Is Firestore?

Firestore is a cloud-hosted, serverless database that stores data in a hierarchical structure of documents and collections. It is a part of the Firebase suite of tools and provides the following benefits:

- **Real-time Synchronization**: Like Firebase Realtime Database, Firestore offers real-time data synchronization, ensuring that changes to data are immediately reflected in connected clients.

- **NoSQL Data Model**: Firestore uses a NoSQL data model, making it suitable for flexible and dynamic data storage. It does not require a predefined schema, allowing you to adapt to changing data needs.

- **Automatic Scaling**: Firestore automatically handles scaling, ensuring that your application can handle a growing user base and large datasets without manual intervention.

- **Offline Support**: Firestore enables offline access, allowing users to read and write data even when they are offline. Changes made offline are synchronized with the server when the internet connection is reestablished.

- **Strong Security**: You can define security rules to control access to your Firestore database, ensuring that data is only accessible to authorized users.

Key Concepts

To understand Firestore better, let's explore some key concepts:

Documents

Documents are the core units of data in Firestore. Each document represents a set of key-value pairs, similar to a JSON object. Documents are organized within collections.

Collections

Collections are containers for documents. You can think of them as tables in a traditional relational database or folders in a file system. Collections group related documents together.

Fields are individual pieces of data within a document. Each field has a name and a value. Firestore supports various data types for fields, including strings, numbers, booleans, arrays, and nested objects.

Document IDs

Each document in Firestore is identified by a unique document ID. You can either manually specify a custom ID or let Firestore generate one for you.

Data Modeling

Firestore's flexible data model allows you to structure your data in a way that best suits your application. Common data modeling patterns include:

- **Flat Collections**: Storing data in a single flat collection and using document IDs to organize and retrieve data.

- **Subcollections**: Nesting collections within other collections to represent hierarchical data relationships.

- **References**: Storing references to other documents within a document, enabling efficient data retrieval and queries.

Getting Started

To get started with Firestore in your Firebase project, you need to initialize Firebase in your web or mobile application and access Firestore through the Firebase SDK. Here's a simplified example of how to initialize Firestore in a web app:

```javascript
// Initialize Firebase
const firebaseConfig = {
  apiKey: 'YOUR_API_KEY',
  authDomain: 'YOUR_AUTH_DOMAIN',
  projectId: 'YOUR_PROJECT_ID',
};

firebase.initializeApp(firebaseConfig);

// Access Firestore
const firestore = firebase.firestore();
```

With Firestore initialized, you can now start storing and retrieving data from your Firestore database.

Firestore is a powerful tool for managing and synchronizing data in your Firebase-powered applications. In the following sections, we'll dive deeper into Firestore's data modeling, querying capabilities, security rules, and integration with mobile and web apps.

4.2 Data Modeling in Firestore

Data modeling in Firestore is a critical aspect of building a well-structured and efficient database for your application. Firestore's flexible NoSQL data model allows you to design your data schema to match your application's requirements. In this section, we'll explore data modeling concepts and best practices for Firestore.

Collections and Documents

Firestore uses a collection-document data model. Data is organized into collections, which are containers for documents. Each document is a set of key-value pairs, and documents within a collection can have different fields.

Here's a high-level overview of collections and documents:

- **Collections**: Collections are analogous to tables in a relational database or directories in a file system. They group related documents together. For example, you might have a "users" collection to store user profiles.

- **Documents**: Documents are individual records within a collection. Each document has a unique ID within its collection. For instance, a "users" collection might contain documents representing individual users.

Document IDs

Firestore automatically generates a unique ID for each document when you create it. You can also provide a custom ID if you want more control over document naming.

```javascript
// Add a document with an auto-generated ID
const newDocRef = firestore.collection('users').add({
  name: 'John Doe',
  email: 'john@example.com',
});

// Add a document with a custom ID
const customDocRef = firestore.collection('products').doc('product123');
```

Subcollections

Firestore allows you to create subcollections within documents. This is useful for representing hierarchical data structures. For example, within a user document, you might have a "posts" subcollection to store the user's posts.

```javascript
// Reference to a subcollection within a user document
const postsCollectionRef = firestore.collection('users').doc('user123').colle
ction('posts');
```

Firestore supports nested data structures, allowing you to store complex data within a document. You can use objects or maps to represent nested data.

```
// Example of nested data within a document
const userDocRef = firestore.collection('users').doc('user123');
userDocRef.set({
  name: 'Alice',
  address: {
    street: '123 Main St',
    city: 'Cityville',
    zip: '12345',
  },
});
```

References and Relationships

In Firestore, you can represent relationships between documents using references. A reference is essentially a link to another document. For instance, if you want to associate a product with a user, you can store a reference to the user's document within the product document.

```
// Storing a reference to a user in a product document
const productDocRef = firestore.collection('products').doc('product123');
const userDocRef = firestore.collection('users').doc('user123');
productDocRef.set({
  name: 'Product A',
  owner: userDocRef,
});
```

Choosing Data Structure

When designing your data model in Firestore, consider the following factors:

- **Query Efficiency**: Choose a data structure that allows efficient querying for your application's use cases. Firestore's querying capabilities are based on the structure of your data.

- **Scalability**: Ensure that your data model scales with your application's growth. Firestore can handle large collections and documents, but efficient querying is essential.

- **Security**: Design your data model with security rules in mind. Restrict access to sensitive data and enforce rules that align with your data structure.

- **Complexity**: Keep your data structure as simple as possible while meeting your application's requirements. Complex data models can be harder to maintain and query.

Firestore's flexible data modeling capabilities enable you to design your database to suit your specific application needs. Whether you're building a simple user profile store or a complex multi-level data hierarchy, Firestore provides the tools to create a structured and efficient database.

4.3 Queries and Transactions

Firestore offers powerful querying capabilities that allow you to retrieve data from your database based on specific criteria. In this section, we'll explore how to perform queries in Firestore and how transactions can help maintain data consistency.

Basic Queries

Firestore allows you to perform various types of queries, including:

- **Get all documents in a collection**: You can retrieve all documents from a specific collection without any filtering.

```javascript
const usersCollectionRef = firestore.collection('users');

// Get all documents in the 'users' collection
usersCollectionRef.get()
  .then((querySnapshot) => {
    querySnapshot.forEach((doc) => {
      console.log(doc.id, '=>', doc.data());
    });
  })
  .catch((error) => {
    console.error('Error getting documents:', error);
  });
```

- **Filtering by field value**: You can filter documents based on the value of a specific field.

```javascript
// Get users with the name 'Alice'
usersCollectionRef.where('name', '==', 'Alice').get()
  .then((querySnapshot) => {
    querySnapshot.forEach((doc) => {
      console.log(doc.id, '=>', doc.data());
    });
  })
  .catch((error) => {
    console.error('Error getting documents:', error);
  });
```

- **Sorting results**: You can order query results based on a specific field.

```javascript
// Get users sorted by age in descending order
usersCollectionRef.orderBy('age', 'desc').get()
```

```javascript
  .then((querySnapshot) => {
    querySnapshot.forEach((doc) => {
      console.log(doc.id, '=>', doc.data());
    });
  })
  .catch((error) => {
    console.error('Error getting documents:', error);
  });
```

- **Limiting results**: You can limit the number of documents returned by a query.

```javascript
// Get the first 5 users
usersCollectionRef.limit(5).get()
  .then((querySnapshot) => {
    querySnapshot.forEach((doc) => {
      console.log(doc.id, '=>', doc.data());
    });
  })
  .catch((error) => {
    console.error('Error getting documents:', error);
  });
```

Compound Queries

Firestore also supports compound queries, which allow you to combine multiple conditions in a single query. For example, you can retrieve documents that match multiple criteria simultaneously.

```javascript
// Get users named 'Alice' who are older than 30
usersCollectionRef.where('name', '==', 'Alice')
  .where('age', '>', 30)
  .get()
  .then((querySnapshot) => {
    querySnapshot.forEach((doc) => {
      console.log(doc.id, '=>', doc.data());
    });
  })
  .catch((error) => {
    console.error('Error getting documents:', error);
  });
```

Transactions

Firestore provides support for transactions to ensure data consistency in situations where multiple clients may be simultaneously updating the same data. Transactions are useful for operations like incrementing counters, updating values based on previous data, or making multiple changes atomically.

Here's an example of a transaction that increments a counter:

```javascript
const counterDocRef = firestore.collection('counters').doc('counter1');
```

```javascript
// Run a transaction to increment the counter
firestore.runTransaction((transaction) => {
  return transaction.get(counterDocRef)
    .then((doc) => {
      if (!doc.exists) {
        throw new Error('Counter document does not exist.');
      }

      const currentCount = doc.data().count || 0;
      const newCount = currentCount + 1;
      transaction.update(counterDocRef, { count: newCount });

      return newCount;
    });
})
.then((newCount) => {
  console.log('Counter incremented to', newCount);
})
.catch((error) => {
  console.error('Transaction failed:', error);
});
```

In this example, the transaction ensures that the counter is incremented correctly even if multiple clients are trying to increment it simultaneously. If a conflict occurs, Firestore will automatically retry the transaction.

Firestore's querying and transaction capabilities empower you to retrieve and manipulate data in your database efficiently and reliably. Whether you need to retrieve specific documents, filter data based on criteria, or maintain data integrity with transactions, Firestore provides the tools you need to work with your data effectively.

4.4 Firestore Security Rules and Indexes

Firestore security rules are a crucial component of ensuring the security and integrity of your data. They allow you to control who can access your data and what operations they can perform. In this section, we'll delve into Firestore security rules and how to set up indexes to optimize your queries.

Firestore Security Rules

Firestore security rules are written in a custom declarative language that resembles JSON. These rules are applied to your data and determine whether a read or write operation is allowed. Firestore rules are evaluated on the server when a client attempts to access the database, ensuring that your data remains secure.

Here's an example of Firestore security rules that restrict access to a "users" collection:

```
rules_version = '2';
service cloud.firestore {
  match /databases/{database}/documents {
    match /users/{userId} {
      allow read, write: if request.auth != null && request.auth.uid == userI
d;
    }
  }
}
```

In this example:

- `rules_version = '2'` specifies the rules format.

- `match /databases/{database}/documents` is the root of the database.

- `match /users/{userId}` defines a rule for the "users" collection and its documents.

- `allow read, write: if ...` specifies the conditions under which reading and writing are allowed. In this case, it allows access only if the client is authenticated (`request.auth != null`) and the authenticated user's UID matches the document's ID.

Firestore security rules are highly flexible and allow you to create complex conditions to match your application's requirements. You can use variables, functions, and operators to define your rules precisely.

Indexes in Firestore

Firestore automatically indexes fields that you use in your queries. However, you may need to set up composite indexes for more complex queries, especially when filtering or sorting based on multiple fields. Firestore enforces these indexes to ensure efficient query execution.

To create a composite index, you can define it in your Firestore security rules, Firebase CLI, or the Firebase Console. Here's how to define a composite index in the Firebase CLI:

```
firebase firestore:indexes

# Then follow the prompts to create an index
```

Firestore indexes are essential for query performance. Without the appropriate indexes, queries may result in slow performance or even fail to execute. Firestore provides tools to identify and create the necessary indexes to support your queries effectively.

Best Practices for Security Rules and Indexes

Here are some best practices for Firestore security rules and indexes:

1. **Keep Rules Simple**: Write rules that are easy to understand and maintain. Complex rules can be error-prone.

2. **Test Rules**: Use the Firebase Security Rules Simulator to test your rules thoroughly before deploying them to production.

3. **Least Privilege**: Only grant the minimum required permissions to users. Follow the principle of least privilege to ensure data security.

4. **Use Variables and Functions**: Leverage variables and functions in your rules to simplify conditions and improve readability.

5. **Monitor and Audit**: Regularly monitor and audit your security rules to ensure they meet your application's needs and security requirements.

Indexes:

1. **Plan Ahead**: Anticipate the types of queries your application will perform and create indexes accordingly.

2. **Avoid Over-Indexing**: Don't create unnecessary indexes, as they can impact write performance and increase costs.

3. **Use the Firebase Console**: Use the Firebase Console or Firebase CLI to create and manage indexes efficiently.

4. **Review Performance**: Periodically review query performance and adjust indexes as needed to maintain optimal performance.

Firestore's security rules and indexing capabilities play a critical role in ensuring data security and query performance. By following best practices for both security rules and indexes, you can create a robust and efficient Firestore database for your application.

4.5 Integrating Firestore with Mobile and Web Apps

Integrating Firestore with your mobile and web applications is a crucial step in leveraging the power of Firebase for real-time data synchronization and storage. In this section, we'll explore how to set up Firestore in your applications, interact with the database, and handle real-time updates.

Setting Up Firestore in Your Application

To get started with Firestore in your mobile or web application, you need to initialize Firebase and access Firestore through the Firebase SDK. Below are the basic steps for setting up Firestore:

1. **Install Firebase SDK**: Add the Firebase SDK to your project using the dependency management system for your platform (e.g., Gradle for Android, CocoaPods for iOS).

2. **Initialize Firebase**: Initialize Firebase in your app by providing your Firebase project configuration. You can obtain this configuration from the Firebase Console.

3. **Access Firestore**: Access Firestore through the Firebase SDK and start using it in your app.

```swift
// Swift (iOS)
import Firebase
FirebaseApp.configure()

let firestore = Firestore.firestore()
```

```java
// Java (Android)
import com.google.firebase.FirebaseApp;
import com.google.firebase.firestore.FirebaseFirestore;

FirebaseApp.initializeApp(this);
FirebaseFirestore firestore = FirebaseFirestore.getInstance();
```

Web Integration:

1. **Add Firebase to Your Web App**: Include the Firebase JavaScript library in your web project using a script tag or a package manager like npm or yarn.

2. **Initialize Firebase**: Initialize Firebase in your web app by providing your Firebase project configuration.

```javascript
// Initialize Firebase
const firebaseConfig = {
  apiKey: 'YOUR_API_KEY',
  authDomain: 'YOUR_AUTH_DOMAIN',
  projectId: 'YOUR_PROJECT_ID',
};

firebase.initializeApp(firebaseConfig);

// Access Firestore
const firestore = firebase.firestore();
```

CRUD Operations in Firestore

Firestore supports basic CRUD (Create, Read, Update, Delete) operations for managing data in your app. Here's an overview of how to perform these operations:

Create (Add) Documents:
```javascript
// Add a new document to a collection
const newDocRef = firestore.collection('users').add({
```

```javascript
  name: 'John Doe',
  email: 'john@example.com',
});
```

Read (Retrieve) Documents:

```javascript
// Get a single document by its ID
const userDocRef = firestore.collection('users').doc('user123');
userDocRef.get()
  .then((doc) => {
    if (doc.exists) {
      console.log(doc.id, '=>', doc.data());
    } else {
      console.log('Document not found.');
    }
  })
  .catch((error) => {
    console.error('Error getting document:', error);
  });
```

Update Documents:

```javascript
// Update an existing document
const userDocRef = firestore.collection('users').doc('user123');
userDocRef.update({
  name: 'Alice',
});
```

Delete Documents:

```javascript
// Delete a document
const userDocRef = firestore.collection('users').doc('user123');
userDocRef.delete()
  .then(() => {
    console.log('Document successfully deleted.');
  })
  .catch((error) => {
    console.error('Error deleting document:', error);
  });
```

Real-Time Updates

One of Firestore's powerful features is real-time data synchronization. You can listen for changes to documents or collections and receive real-time updates whenever data changes. This is particularly useful for building interactive and collaborative applications.

Here's an example of how to listen for real-time updates to a document:

```javascript
const userDocRef = firestore.collection('users').doc('user123');
userDocRef.onSnapshot((doc) => {
  if (doc.exists) {
    console.log('Document data:', doc.data());
  } else {
    console.log('Document removed.');
```

```
  }
});
```


Firestore also provides offline support, allowing your app to read and write data even when there is no internet connection. Firestore automatically queues up changes made offline and syncs them with the server when the connection is reestablished.

Firestore's seamless integration with mobile and web platforms, real-time updates, and offline support make it a powerful choice for managing data in your applications. Whether you're building a mobile app, web app, or both, Firestore provides a robust and scalable solution for storing and synchronizing data.

Chapter 5: Firebase Storage

5.1 Introduction to Cloud Storage in Firebase

Firebase Storage is a powerful cloud storage solution provided by Firebase, allowing you to store and serve user-generated content such as images, videos, and other files. It integrates seamlessly with other Firebase services and provides secure, scalable, and cost-effective storage for your mobile and web applications.

Key Features of Firebase Storage

Firebase Storage offers several key features that make it a valuable asset for developers:

1. **User-Friendly SDK**: Firebase provides SDKs for various platforms, including iOS, Android, and web, making it easy to integrate cloud storage into your applications.

2. **Security Rules**: Just like Firestore, Firebase Storage allows you to define security rules to control who can upload, download, or delete files. You can define rules based on user authentication, data validation, and more.

3. **File Metadata**: You can store metadata alongside your files, such as timestamps, user information, or custom data. This metadata can be useful for organizing and managing your content.

4. **Large File Support**: Firebase Storage can handle large files, making it suitable for applications that deal with media assets like high-resolution images or video files.

5. **Image Thumbnails**: Firebase Storage can automatically generate thumbnails for images, helping you optimize bandwidth and load times when displaying images in your app.

6. **Data Transfer Costs**: Firebase Storage offers cost-effective data transfer pricing, which can help reduce your application's operating costs.

7. **Integration with Firebase**: Firebase Storage seamlessly integrates with other Firebase services, such as Firebase Authentication, Firestore, and Firebase Realtime Database, enabling a comprehensive backend solution for your app.

Getting Started with Firebase Storage

To use Firebase Storage in your application, you'll need to set up Firebase and enable the Firebase Storage service for your project. Here are the basic steps to get started:

1. **Create a Firebase Project**: If you haven't already, create a Firebase project in the Firebase Console (https://console.firebase.google.com/).

2. **Initialize Firebase**: Initialize Firebase in your mobile or web app by adding the Firebase SDK and configuration. This is similar to what you did for Firestore integration.

3. **Enable Firebase Storage**: In the Firebase Console, navigate to the Storage section and enable Firebase Storage for your project.

4. **Upload Files**: You can now start uploading files to Firebase Storage using the SDK for your platform. Here's an example of how to upload a file in JavaScript (for web):

```javascript
// Get a reference to the storage service
const storage = firebase.storage();

// Create a storage reference
const storageRef = storage.ref();

// Upload a file
const fileInput = document.getElementById('fileInput');
const file = fileInput.files[0];
const fileRef = storageRef.child('images/' + file.name);
fileRef.put(file).then((snapshot) => {
  console.log('Uploaded a file!');
});
```

5. **Download Files**: You can also download files from Firebase Storage using the SDK. Here's an example:

```javascript
// Download a file
const fileRef = storageRef.child('images/image.jpg');
fileRef.getDownloadURL().then((url) => {
  // Use the URL to display or download the file
  console.log('File URL:', url);
});
```

Use Cases for Firebase Storage

Firebase Storage can be used for various purposes in your application, including:

- Storing and serving user profile pictures.
- Hosting media files for a content-sharing app.
- Storing user-generated content like images or videos.
- Hosting files for a document management system.
- Storing and serving assets for a web app or game.

Firebase Storage provides a reliable and scalable solution for managing and serving files in your Firebase-powered applications, reducing the complexity of building and maintaining your own file storage infrastructure.

5.2 Uploading and Retrieving Files

Firebase Storage simplifies the process of uploading and retrieving files in your mobile and web applications. In this section, we'll explore how to upload files to Firebase Storage and retrieve them for use in your app.

Uploading Files to Firebase Storage

To upload a file to Firebase Storage, follow these steps:

1. **Initialize Firebase Storage**: Ensure that Firebase Storage is initialized in your app. You can do this by including the Firebase SDK and configuring it with your Firebase project credentials, as mentioned in the previous section.

2. **Select a File**: Allow users to select a file they want to upload. This can be done using HTML file input elements for web apps or file pickers in mobile apps.

3. **Create a Storage Reference**: Create a reference to the location in Firebase Storage where you want to store the file. You can use the `storage().ref()` method to create a reference to the root of your storage bucket or specify a subdirectory.

4. **Upload the File**: Use the `put()` method to upload the selected file to Firebase Storage. This method takes the reference and the file as parameters and returns a `UploadTask` object, which you can use to monitor the upload progress or handle completion.

Here's an example of how to upload a file in a web app:

```javascript
// Get a reference to the storage service
const storage = firebase.storage();

// Create a storage reference
const storageRef = storage.ref();

// Select a file using an input element
const fileInput = document.getElementById('fileInput');
const file = fileInput.files[0];

// Create a reference to the location where you want to store the file
const fileRef = storageRef.child('images/' + file.name);

// Upload the file
const uploadTask = fileRef.put(file);

// Monitor the upload progress
uploadTask.on('state_changed', (snapshot) => {
  // Handle progress, errors, and completion here
}, (error) => {
  // Handle errors
}, () => {
```

```javascript
  // Upload completed successfully
  console.log('File uploaded!');
});
```


Retrieving Files from Firebase Storage

Once you have uploaded files to Firebase Storage, you can retrieve and use them in your app. Here's how to retrieve files:

1. **Create a Storage Reference**: To retrieve a file, create a reference to the location of the file in Firebase Storage using the `storage().ref()` method.

2. **Download the File**: Use the `getDownloadURL()` method on the reference to obtain a secure URL that allows you to download the file. This URL can be used to display or download the file in your app.

Here's an example of how to retrieve a file in a web app:

```javascript
// Create a reference to the location of the file you want to retrieve
const fileRef = storageRef.child('images/image.jpg');

// Get the download URL for the file
fileRef.getDownloadURL().then((url) => {
  // Use the URL to display or download the file
  console.log('File URL:', url);
}).catch((error) => {
  // Handle errors
  console.error('Error getting download URL:', error);
});
```

File Metadata

Firebase Storage allows you to store metadata alongside your files, which can include information like timestamps, user data, or custom attributes. Metadata can be useful for organizing and managing your content.

You can set and retrieve metadata for files when uploading or updating them. Here's an example of setting metadata during the upload process:

```javascript
// Set custom metadata for the uploaded file
const metadata = {
  customMetadata: {
    createdBy: 'John Doe',
    uploadDate: new Date().toString(),
  },
};

// Upload the file with metadata
const uploadTask = fileRef.put(file, metadata);
```

You can also retrieve file metadata using the `getMetadata()` method on a storage reference:

```
// Get metadata for a file
fileRef.getMetadata().then((metadata) => {
  // Access metadata properties
  console.log('File metadata:', metadata);
}).catch((error) => {
  // Handle errors
  console.error('Error getting metadata:', error);
});
```

Firebase Storage's straightforward API makes it easy to upload and retrieve files, and the ability to attach metadata provides additional flexibility for managing your content. Whether you're building an image-sharing app, a document storage solution, or handling user-generated content, Firebase Storage can simplify the process of file management in your app.

5.3 Managing User-Generated Content

Firebase Storage is an excellent solution for managing user-generated content in your mobile and web applications. In this section, we'll explore various strategies and best practices for efficiently managing and serving user-generated content using Firebase Storage.

User-Generated Content Types

User-generated content (UGC) can encompass a wide range of media and file types, including images, videos, audio files, documents, and more. Firebase Storage can accommodate these various content types and provides the flexibility to store and serve them seamlessly.

Organizing User-Generated Content

Efficiently organizing user-generated content is essential for easy retrieval and management. Firebase Storage allows you to structure your content storage based on your application's requirements. Common organizational strategies include:

1. **Hierarchical Structure**: Use folders or directories to organize content based on categories, users, or dates. For example, you can create folders for each user's uploads or categorize content by content type.

2. **File Naming Conventions**: Implement consistent and descriptive file naming conventions. This makes it easier to identify and locate specific files.

3. **Metadata**: Leverage metadata to store additional information about each file, such as timestamps, user data, or custom attributes. This metadata can help with content organization and retrieval.

When managing user-generated content, it's crucial to enforce security rules to protect your data and control access to files. Firebase Storage allows you to define security rules that specify who can upload, download, or delete files.

Here's an example of security rules that restrict access to user-specific folders:

```
rules_version = '2';
service firebase.storage {
  match /b/{bucket}/o {
    match /user_content/{userId}/{allPaths=**} {
      allow read, write: if request.auth != null && request.auth.uid == userI
d;
    }
  }
}
```

In this example:

- `match /b/{bucket}/o` specifies the root of the storage bucket.

- `match /user_content/{userId}/{allPaths=**}` defines a rule for user-specific folders and their contents.

- `allow read, write: if ...` specifies that only authenticated users with matching user IDs can read and write to their own folders.

When dealing with user-generated content, it's essential to consider the potential size of files and scalability. Firebase Storage can handle large files, but you should be mindful of the following:

1. **File Size Limitations**: Firebase Storage has a maximum file size limit (e.g., 2 GB per file). Ensure that your application handles large files appropriately and considers user experience.

2. **Optimizing File Uploads**: Implement mechanisms to optimize file uploads, such as resumable uploads, to handle interruptions and large files efficiently.

3. **CDN Integration**: Firebase Storage leverages Content Delivery Networks (CDNs) for serving content, ensuring fast and scalable delivery to users globally.

If your application allows users to interact with and comment on user-generated content, consider implementing real-time updates using Firebase Realtime Database or Firestore. This enables real-time notifications and collaboration features, enhancing user engagement.

File Deletion and Cleanup

Implement a strategy for managing file deletion and cleanup to ensure that unused or outdated user-generated content is removed from Firebase Storage. You can use cloud functions and scheduled tasks to automate this process based on your application's requirements.

Managing user-generated content is a crucial aspect of many applications, from social media platforms to document management systems. Firebase Storage provides the tools and flexibility you need to efficiently store, secure, and serve user-generated content while adhering to best practices for organization, security, and scalability.

5.4 Implementing Security Rules for Storage

Implementing proper security rules in Firebase Storage is crucial to safeguard your user-generated content and ensure that unauthorized users cannot access, modify, or delete files. In this section, we'll dive into how to define and implement security rules effectively.

Anatomy of Firebase Storage Security Rules

Firebase Storage security rules are defined using a domain-specific language (DSL) that allows you to specify who can access which parts of your storage bucket. The rules are structured as follows:

```
rules_version = '2';
service firebase.storage {
  match /b/{bucket}/o {
    // Rules for storage paths go here
  }
}
```

- `rules_version` indicates the version of the rules language. In this example, it's set to '2', which is the latest version.

- `service firebase.storage` specifies that these rules apply to Firebase Storage.

- `match /b/{bucket}/o` is the root of the storage bucket where you define rules for specific storage paths.

One of the fundamental principles of Firebase Storage security is controlling access based on user authentication. You can restrict access to authenticated users or specific user groups by using the `request.auth` object, which contains user authentication information.

Here's an example of a security rule that allows read and write access only to authenticated users:

```
rules_version = '2';
service firebase.storage {
  match /b/{bucket}/o {
    match /user_content/{userId}/{allPaths=**} {
      allow read, write: if request.auth != null;
    }
  }
}
```

In this rule:

- `request.auth != null` checks if the request is made by an authenticated user.

- `{allPaths=**}` matches all files and subdirectories within the specified path.

Using Custom Claims for Fine-Grained Access Control

Firebase Authentication allows you to assign custom claims to users, which can be used for fine-grained access control in storage security rules. Custom claims can represent user roles, permissions, or any additional user attributes you want to leverage.

Here's an example of using custom claims to control access:

```
rules_version = '2';
service firebase.storage {
  match /b/{bucket}/o {
    match /admin_content/{allPaths=**} {
      allow read, write: if request.auth != null && request.auth.token.admin == true;
    }
  }
}
```

In this rule:

- `request.auth.token.admin == true` checks if the user has the admin custom claim set to `true`.

- `match /admin_content/{allPaths=**}` specifies the path where this rule applies.

When dealing with sensitive user-generated content or data, you may need to enforce stricter security rules. For example, you can restrict access to files containing personal information or confidential data to specific user roles or administrators only.

Here's an example of protecting sensitive files with security rules:

```
rules_version = '2';
service firebase.storage {
  match /b/{bucket}/o {
    match /sensitive_data/{userId}/{allPaths=**} {
      allow read, write: if request.auth != null && (
        request.auth.uid == userId || request.auth.token.admin == true
      );
    }
  }
}
```

In this rule:

- `request.auth.uid == userId` allows the owner of the sensitive data to read and write.

- `request.auth.token.admin == true` allows administrators to access the data.

Testing and Simulating Security Rules

Firebase provides tools for testing and simulating your security rules to ensure they work as expected. You can use the Firebase Realtime Database Simulator or the Firebase Emulator Suite to test your storage security rules with different scenarios.

Implementing robust security rules is a critical aspect of Firebase Storage configuration. By following best practices and leveraging authentication and custom claims, you can protect user-generated content and sensitive data effectively while ensuring that authorized users can access the resources they need.

5.5 Best Practices for File Handling

Efficiently handling files in Firebase Storage is essential for maintaining a smooth user experience and optimizing your application's performance. In this section, we'll explore some best practices and tips for effectively managing files in Firebase Storage.

1. File Organization

Organize Your Storage Structure: Plan and structure your storage buckets and paths to align with your application's data model. Create a logical hierarchy using folders or directories to keep content organized. Consider categorizing files based on user, content type, or other relevant criteria.

Use Descriptive File Names: Adopt a consistent and descriptive file naming convention. A clear naming convention makes it easier to identify and retrieve files. Include relevant information such as timestamps, user IDs, or content identifiers in file names.

2. Security and Access Control

Implement Strong Security Rules: Define and enforce security rules that protect your files from unauthorized access. Use Firebase Authentication and custom claims to control who can read, write, or delete files. Regularly review and update your security rules to adapt to changing requirements.

Leverage Custom Claims: For fine-grained access control, assign custom claims to users based on their roles or permissions. Use these claims in your security rules to grant or deny access to specific resources. Be cautious when granting elevated privileges to users through custom claims.

3. Metadata Management

Utilize File Metadata: Firebase Storage allows you to attach metadata to files. Leverage this feature to store additional information such as timestamps, user data, or custom attributes. Metadata can assist in organizing and searching for files efficiently.

Retrieve Metadata Efficiently: When retrieving file metadata, consider using batch operations or caching mechanisms to minimize requests to Firebase Storage. This reduces the overhead and improves performance, especially when dealing with a large number of files.

4. Scalability and Performance

Optimize for Scalability: Firebase Storage automatically scales to accommodate your application's needs. However, consider using Content Delivery Networks (CDNs) for content delivery to users, especially for large media files. CDNs can significantly improve file loading times for global audiences.

Resumable Uploads: Implement resumable file uploads to handle interruptions and large file uploads more efficiently. Firebase Storage supports resumable uploads, ensuring that users can complete uploads even if they experience network issues.

5. Cleanup and Deletion

Automate Cleanup: Implement automated processes or cloud functions to clean up and delete unused or outdated files. Regularly review your storage for files that are no longer needed and remove them to free up storage space and reduce costs.

Retention Policies: Define retention policies for your files to determine how long they should be stored. Some files may need to be retained for compliance or auditing purposes, while others can be deleted after a certain period.

Handle Upload and Download Errors: Implement error handling mechanisms to gracefully handle upload and download failures. Provide informative error messages to users when file operations encounter issues.

Monitor Storage Usage: Monitor your storage usage and performance using Firebase Analytics and Firebase Performance Monitoring. This helps you identify bottlenecks, track user engagement with files, and optimize your storage configuration.

7. User Experience

Optimize User Experience: Consider user experience when delivering files. Implement lazy loading for images and videos to improve initial page load times. Provide feedback to users during file upload and download processes, such as progress indicators.

Consider File Compression: Depending on your application's requirements, you may want to implement file compression techniques to reduce file sizes, especially for images and videos. Smaller file sizes lead to faster load times and reduced bandwidth usage.

By following these best practices, you can effectively manage files in Firebase Storage, ensure data security, optimize performance, and provide a seamless user experience. Firebase Storage provides the tools you need to handle user-generated content efficiently, and adhering to these guidelines will help you make the most of this powerful cloud storage solution.

Chapter 6: Firebase Hosting

Section 6.1: Hosting Overview: Static and Dynamic Content

Firebase Hosting is a powerful and user-friendly solution for hosting web applications, websites, and dynamic content on Google's infrastructure. It offers a simple way to deploy and manage web content, making it an ideal choice for developers looking to host their projects, whether they are static websites, single-page applications (SPAs), or server-rendered dynamic sites.

Key Features of Firebase Hosting

Firebase Hosting provides several key features that make it a popular choice among developers:

1. **Global Content Delivery**: Firebase Hosting uses a global Content Delivery Network (CDN) that ensures your web content is served from multiple locations worldwide. This leads to faster loading times for users, regardless of their geographic location.

2. **SSL Support**: Firebase Hosting offers free SSL certificates, enabling secure connections for your websites and applications. This is crucial for user trust and search engine rankings.

3. **Custom Domains**: You can easily configure custom domains for your Firebase-hosted content. This means you can use your own domain names (e.g., www.yourwebsite.com) instead of Firebase's default subdomains.

4. **Rewrites and Redirects**: Firebase Hosting allows you to define URL rewrites and redirects, making it possible to create clean and user-friendly URLs for your application's routes and pages.

5. **Deployment from the Command Line**: Firebase Hosting can be managed and deployed directly from the Firebase Command Line Interface (CLI). This streamlines the development and deployment process.

6. **Rollback**: Firebase Hosting maintains a history of deployments, which enables you to easily roll back to a previous version of your site if needed.

7. **Integration with Firebase Services**: Firebase Hosting seamlessly integrates with other Firebase services, such as Firebase Authentication, Realtime Database, and Cloud Functions, allowing you to build powerful and dynamic web applications.

Static vs. Dynamic Content

Before diving deeper into Firebase Hosting, it's essential to understand the difference between static and dynamic content:

- **Static Content**: Static content consists of files that don't change based on user interactions or database queries. These files include HTML, CSS, JavaScript, images, and other assets. Static sites are typically generated during the build process and served as-is to users.

- **Dynamic Content**: Dynamic content, on the other hand, is generated on-the-fly in response to user requests. It often relies on server-side processing, databases, and user input. Examples include social media feeds, e-commerce product listings, and personalized user profiles.

Firebase Hosting is well-suited for hosting static content and can be combined with Firebase Cloud Functions to serve dynamic content through serverless APIs.

Getting Started with Firebase Hosting

To get started with Firebase Hosting, you'll need to have a Firebase project set up. If you haven't created one yet, refer to Chapter 1, Section 1.4 for instructions on setting up a Firebase project.

Once you have a Firebase project, you can initialize Firebase Hosting for your project using the Firebase CLI. Here are the basic steps:

1. Install the Firebase CLI if you haven't already by running `npm install -g firebase-tools` in your terminal.

2. Authenticate with Firebase by running `firebase login`. This will open a web page where you can sign in with your Google account.

3. Navigate to your project's root directory in the terminal.

4. Run `firebase init hosting`. This command will guide you through the setup process, including configuring your project for Firebase Hosting and specifying your public directory (the folder containing your web assets).

5. Finally, deploy your web content to Firebase Hosting using `firebase deploy`. This will upload your static files to Firebase and make them accessible via a public URL.

Now, your web content is live on Firebase Hosting, and you can access it via the provided URL or your custom domain if you've configured one.

In the following sections, we'll explore advanced topics related to Firebase Hosting, including custom domains, SSL configuration, performance optimization, and more. Firebase Hosting simplifies the deployment process and allows you to focus on building great web experiences for your users.

Section 6.2: Setting Up and Deploying a Project

In Section 6.1, we explored the fundamentals of Firebase Hosting and its benefits. Now, let's delve into the practical aspects of setting up and deploying a web project using Firebase Hosting.

Prerequisites

Before you start, ensure you have the following prerequisites in place:

1. **Firebase CLI**: Install the Firebase Command Line Interface (CLI) globally if you haven't already. You can do this using npm by running `npm install -g firebase-tools`.

2. **Firebase Project**: You should have a Firebase project created. If not, refer to Chapter 1, Section 1.4, for instructions on setting up a Firebase project.

Initialize Firebase Hosting

1. Open your terminal and navigate to the root directory of your web project.

2. Run `firebase login` to authenticate with your Firebase account. This command will open a web page where you can sign in with your Google account.

3. Once authenticated, run `firebase init hosting` to initialize Firebase Hosting for your project. This command will guide you through the setup process.

- You'll be prompted to select an existing Firebase project or create a new one if you haven't already.
- Choose a Firebase Hosting public directory. This is the folder containing your web assets (HTML, CSS, JavaScript, etc.). The default is usually `public`, but you can specify a different directory if needed.

4. After completing the initialization, you'll see a `firebase.json` file in your project directory. This file contains Firebase Hosting configuration settings.

Deploy Your Project

Now that your project is set up for Firebase Hosting, it's time to deploy your web content.

1. Ensure you are in your project's root directory in the terminal.

2. Run `firebase deploy`. This command will upload your static files to Firebase Hosting, and Firebase will provide you with a public URL where your site is accessible.

   ```
   firebase deploy
   ```

3. Once the deployment is complete, Firebase will display the hosting URL in the terminal. You can visit this URL in your web browser to view your deployed site.

Continuous Deployment

Firebase Hosting integrates seamlessly with version control systems like Git, allowing for continuous deployment (CD) workflows. With CD, changes made to your project's repository trigger automatic deployments to Firebase Hosting.

Here's a simplified example of how you can set up continuous deployment with Firebase Hosting and GitHub:

1. **Connect Firebase Hosting to Your Repository**: In the Firebase Console, navigate to your project's Hosting settings. Under the "Continuous Deployment" section, link your GitHub repository.

2. **Configure GitHub Actions (or Other CI/CD Services)**: Set up GitHub Actions to build and deploy your project to Firebase Hosting automatically when changes are pushed to your repository.

3. **Push Code to GitHub**: As you make changes to your project and push them to your GitHub repository, GitHub Actions will automatically trigger the deployment workflow to Firebase Hosting.

This approach streamlines the deployment process, making it easier to collaborate with a team and ensure that the latest version of your web application is always live.

In Section 6.3, we will explore custom domains and SSL configuration, allowing you to personalize your Firebase Hosting setup further and enhance security.

Firebase Hosting offers the flexibility to use custom domains for your web projects, allowing you to personalize the URLs users see when accessing your content. In addition to custom domains, Firebase Hosting provides built-in support for SSL (Secure Sockets Layer) certificates, ensuring that your web traffic is encrypted and secure. Let's explore how to set up custom domains and SSL for your Firebase Hosting project.

Custom Domains

Using a custom domain, such as "www.yourwebsite.com," instead of Firebase's default subdomains, provides a more professional and branded appearance for your web project. Here's how to set up a custom domain:

1. **Purchase a Domain**: You'll need to purchase a domain name from a domain registrar like GoDaddy, Namecheap, Google Domains, or others. Follow the registrar's instructions to purchase the domain.

2. **Configure DNS Records**: After purchasing the domain, configure the DNS (Domain Name System) records to point to Firebase Hosting. Firebase provides detailed instructions on the necessary DNS records to set up. This typically involves creating DNS records like A or CNAME records that point to Firebase's hosting servers.

3. **Verify Domain Ownership**: In the Firebase Console, navigate to your project's Hosting settings. Under the "Custom Domains" section, click on "Add custom domain." Firebase will guide you through the verification process, which may involve adding TXT records to your domain's DNS settings.

4. **Set Up SSL**: After domain verification, Firebase Hosting will automatically provision an SSL certificate for your custom domain, ensuring secure HTTPS connections.

5. **Associate Domain**: Once the domain is verified and SSL is set up, you can associate the custom domain with your Firebase Hosting project. Firebase will provide instructions for this step, typically involving adding a domain alias in your `firebase.json` file.

6. **Deploy Changes**: After associating the custom domain, deploy your project using `firebase deploy`. Firebase will update the hosting configuration with the custom domain settings.

7. **Test Your Custom Domain**: You can now access your Firebase-hosted project using the custom domain. It may take some time for DNS changes to propagate globally, so be patient if the custom domain doesn't work immediately.

Firebase Hosting ensures secure connections by automatically provisioning SSL certificates for your Firebase subdomains and custom domains. SSL certificates enable HTTPS, encrypting data exchanged between users and your web server. Firebase takes care of the SSL configuration and renewal process, making it easy for you to maintain a secure web presence.

Key points about SSL in Firebase Hosting:

- Firebase provides free SSL certificates, eliminating the need for you to purchase or manage them separately.

- SSL certificates are automatically renewed by Firebase Hosting, so you don't have to worry about expiration.

- When you use a custom domain, Firebase Hosting will automatically provision and configure SSL for it, ensuring that your users can access your site securely via HTTPS.

- SSL is essential not only for security but also for SEO (Search Engine Optimization). Search engines prioritize HTTPS websites, which can improve your site's search engine rankings.

By using custom domains and SSL certificates in Firebase Hosting, you can enhance the user experience, build trust with your audience, and improve the security and visibility of your web projects.

In Section 6.4, we will explore performance optimization and Content Delivery Network (CDN) integration to ensure that your Firebase-hosted content loads quickly and efficiently for users around the world.

Section 6.4: Performance Optimization and CDN Integration

Performance is a critical aspect of any web application. Users expect fast-loading content, and slow websites can lead to high bounce rates and a poor user experience. Firebase Hosting offers built-in tools and features to optimize the performance of your web projects and leverage Content Delivery Networks (CDNs) for faster content delivery worldwide.

Content Delivery Network (CDN) Integration

A Content Delivery Network (CDN) is a network of distributed servers strategically placed in various locations worldwide. CDNs work by caching and delivering content to users from the server closest to their geographic location. Firebase Hosting seamlessly integrates with a global CDN, ensuring that your web content is delivered quickly to users regardless of their location.

Here's how Firebase Hosting's CDN integration benefits your web projects:

1. **Reduced Latency**: With CDN integration, users receive content from a server geographically closer to them. This reduces the time it takes to fetch and display your web pages, resulting in faster load times.

2. **Improved Reliability**: CDNs enhance the reliability of your web projects by distributing content across multiple servers. Even if one server experiences issues, the CDN automatically routes traffic to the next available server, minimizing downtime.

3. **Traffic Scalability**: CDNs are designed to handle high levels of traffic. As your web project grows and experiences increased user activity, the CDN can efficiently scale to accommodate the demand.

4. **Global Reach**: Firebase Hosting's CDN has servers located worldwide. This means your content can be delivered to users across the globe with minimal latency, providing a consistent and fast user experience for an international audience.

To leverage Firebase Hosting's CDN integration, you don't need to configure anything manually; it's built into the service. Firebase Hosting automatically distributes your content across its global network of servers, optimizing performance for your users.

Performance Optimization

While Firebase Hosting's CDN takes care of a significant part of performance optimization, there are additional best practices you can follow to ensure that your web projects load quickly and efficiently:

1. **Compress Assets**: Compress images, CSS, and JavaScript files to reduce their file sizes. Smaller files load faster, especially on slower internet connections.

2. **Use Browser Caching**: Set appropriate cache headers for your static assets to allow browsers to cache them locally. This reduces the need to re-download assets on subsequent visits.

3. **Minify Code**: Minify your CSS and JavaScript code by removing unnecessary whitespace and comments. Minified code is smaller and quicker to load.

4. **Lazy Load Images**: Implement lazy loading for images so that they load only when they come into the user's viewport, saving bandwidth and improving page load times.

5. **Optimize Critical Rendering Path**: Prioritize rendering of above-the-fold content to ensure that users see meaningful content quickly.

6. **Monitor Performance**: Use performance monitoring tools like Firebase Performance Monitoring (covered in Chapter 9) to identify and address bottlenecks and slow-loading components.

7. **Test and Iterate**: Regularly test your web projects using tools like Google PageSpeed Insights or Lighthouse to identify areas for improvement. Implement changes and iterate to achieve optimal performance.

By integrating a CDN and following performance optimization best practices, you can provide a smooth and responsive user experience, regardless of your web project's complexity or global reach.

In Section 6.5, we will explore how to leverage Firebase Hosting for scalability, ensuring that your web projects can handle traffic spikes and growing user bases.

Section 6.5: Leveraging Firebase Hosting for Scalability

Firebase Hosting offers powerful scalability features that ensure your web projects can handle increasing traffic and growing user bases. As your web application gains popularity, it's crucial to have a hosting solution that can seamlessly scale to meet demand without compromising performance or reliability. In this section, we'll explore how Firebase Hosting can help you achieve scalability.

Automatic Scaling

Firebase Hosting automatically handles the scaling of your web projects. It employs a global Content Delivery Network (CDN) to distribute your content to users worldwide, ensuring low-latency access regardless of their geographic location. Firebase's infrastructure is designed to handle traffic spikes and maintain responsiveness, even during high-demand periods.

Key features of Firebase Hosting's automatic scaling:

1. **Global CDN**: Firebase Hosting's integration with a global CDN ensures that your content is cached and served from servers strategically located worldwide. This minimizes the load on your origin server and reduces latency for users.

2. **Traffic Handling**: Whether you experience a sudden surge in traffic due to a viral campaign or ongoing organic growth, Firebase Hosting dynamically scales to accommodate the increased load. This means your web projects remain responsive and available even during traffic spikes.

3. **Load Balancing**: Firebase Hosting employs load balancing techniques to evenly distribute traffic across its infrastructure. This prevents any single server from becoming a bottleneck, ensuring consistent performance.

4. **DDoS Protection**: Firebase Hosting includes built-in DDoS (Distributed Denial of Service) protection to mitigate and block malicious traffic, further enhancing your web project's availability and reliability.

Firebase Hosting's automatic scaling also offers cost-effective scalability. You only pay for the resources you consume, which means that during periods of low traffic, you won't be overpaying for idle server capacity. Firebase's pay-as-you-go pricing model allows you to scale up or down based on actual usage, optimizing your hosting costs.

Traffic Control

Firebase Hosting provides traffic control mechanisms that allow you to manage and route traffic based on various criteria. These features can help you further optimize the scalability of your web projects:

1. **A/B Testing**: Conduct A/B tests to assess the impact of different versions of your website or app. Firebase Hosting allows you to divert a percentage of your traffic to alternative versions and measure user engagement and conversion rates.

2. **Feature Flags**: Implement feature flags to control the availability of specific features within your web project. This can help you gradually roll out new features to a subset of users or quickly disable features if issues arise.

3. **Rollbacks**: If a new release introduces unexpected issues or bugs, Firebase Hosting makes it easy to roll back to a previous version, ensuring minimal disruption to your users.

By leveraging Firebase Hosting's automatic scaling, cost-effective pricing, and traffic control features, you can confidently handle traffic spikes and accommodate a growing user base while maintaining a high level of performance and reliability.

In the next chapter, we will dive into Firebase Cloud Functions, which enable you to add serverless functionality to your web projects, further enhancing their capabilities and scalability.

Chapter 7: Firebase Functions

Section 7.1: Introduction to Cloud Functions

Firebase Functions, also known as Cloud Functions for Firebase, is a serverless computing service that allows you to run custom backend code in response to events in your Firebase ecosystem. These events can include changes to your Firebase Realtime Database, Firestore, authentication events, or even HTTP requests. Firebase Functions simplify backend development by allowing you to focus on writing code that responds to specific events without worrying about managing servers or infrastructure.

Key Concepts

Before diving into the details of Firebase Functions, let's explore some key concepts:

1. **Serverless Computing**: Firebase Functions follow the serverless computing paradigm. This means you don't need to provision or manage servers. Firebase automatically handles the infrastructure, scaling, and execution of your code in response to events.

2. **Event-Driven**: Firebase Functions are triggered by events. These events can originate from various sources within Firebase, such as Realtime Database changes, Firestore document updates, authentication events, Cloud Storage uploads, and HTTP requests. When a specified event occurs, your function is executed.

3. **Event Handlers**: Firebase Functions act as event handlers. You write JavaScript or TypeScript code that defines how your function should respond to specific events. For example, you can create a function that sends a welcome email to a user when they sign up.

4. **Asynchronous Execution**: Firebase Functions are designed to perform tasks asynchronously. This means they can execute in the background without blocking the main application thread. Asynchronous execution is particularly useful for tasks like sending notifications or processing data.

5. **Triggers and Actions**: In Firebase Functions, events are associated with triggers, and triggers lead to actions. For instance, you can set up a trigger that listens for new Firestore document creations and specify an action that sends a notification to a user when a new document is added.

Use Cases

Firebase Functions can enhance the functionality of your Firebase-powered applications in various ways:

1. **Realtime Updates**: You can use Firebase Functions to listen for changes in your Realtime Database or Firestore. This enables real-time updates in your web or mobile applications when data changes on the server.

2. **Authentication**: Implement custom authentication logic, such as sending a verification email when a user signs up or updating user profiles.

3. **Notifications**: Send push notifications to users when certain events occur, like receiving a new message or a friend request.

4. **Data Processing**: Process and transform data as it is added or updated in your database. For example, you can automatically generate thumbnails for uploaded images.

5. **Integration**: Connect your Firebase application with external services or APIs by using Firebase Functions as intermediaries to handle data synchronization or other tasks.

Firebase Functions can be a powerful tool in your Firebase development toolkit, allowing you to add custom backend logic and automation to your applications without the overhead of managing servers.

In the following sections of this chapter, we will explore how to write, deploy, and manage Firebase Functions, as well as their integration with other Firebase services and third-party APIs.

Section 7.2: Writing and Deploying Functions

In this section, we will delve into the process of writing and deploying Firebase Functions. Firebase provides a straightforward way to write serverless functions that respond to various events within your Firebase project. These events can be anything from changes in your database to user authentication actions or even HTTP requests.

Writing Firebase Functions

Firebase Functions are typically written in JavaScript or TypeScript. Here's a simple example of a Firebase Function written in JavaScript:

```javascript
const functions = require('firebase-functions');

// Define a function that responds to an HTTP request
exports.helloWorld = functions.https.onRequest((request, response) => {
  response.send('Hello, Firebase!');
});

// Define a function that triggers on a Firestore document creation
exports.notifyUser = functions.firestore
  .document('users/{userId}')
  .onCreate((snapshot, context) => {
    const userId = context.params.userId;
```

```javascript
    console.log(`New user with ID ${userId} created.`);
    // You can perform actions like sending notifications here
    return null;
  });
});
```

In this example, we define two Firebase Functions:

1. `helloWorld`: This function responds to an HTTP request with a simple "Hello, Firebase!" message.

2. `notifyUser`: This function triggers when a new document is created in the Firestore collection 'users.' It logs a message and can perform additional actions, such as sending notifications.

You can also write Firebase Functions in TypeScript for better type safety and tooling support. Firebase provides TypeScript typings for Firebase services, making it easier to work with Firestore, Realtime Database, and other Firebase components.

Deploying Firebase Functions

Once you've written your Firebase Functions, you can deploy them to Firebase's serverless infrastructure. Here's how to deploy functions using the Firebase CLI:

1. Install the Firebase CLI if you haven't already by running `npm install -g firebase-tools`.

2. Log in to your Firebase account using `firebase login`.

3. Navigate to your Firebase project's root directory in the terminal.

4. Deploy your functions using `firebase deploy --only functions`.

Firebase will deploy your functions to the cloud, making them available to respond to events as specified.

Triggering Firebase Functions

Firebase Functions can be triggered by various types of events:

- **Firestore Triggers**: You can trigger functions when documents in Firestore are created, updated, or deleted.

- **Realtime Database Triggers**: Similar to Firestore, functions can respond to changes in the Realtime Database.

- **Authentication Triggers**: Firebase Functions can be triggered when users sign up, log in, or other authentication-related events occur.

- **HTTP Triggers**: You can expose functions as HTTP endpoints, allowing them to be invoked via HTTP requests.

- **Cloud Storage Triggers**: Functions can be triggered when files are uploaded, updated, or deleted in Firebase Cloud Storage.

By understanding how to write and deploy Firebase Functions, you gain the ability to add custom logic and automation to your Firebase project, enhancing its capabilities and responsiveness. In the next section, we will explore serverless architecture with Firebase and how to build powerful backend solutions using Firebase Functions.

Section 7.3: Serverless Architecture with Firebase

Firebase Functions are a key component of serverless architecture. Serverless architecture, sometimes referred to as Function as a Service (FaaS), allows developers to build and run applications without managing servers. Firebase Functions, in particular, enable you to create serverless backend code that responds to events, and they seamlessly integrate with other Firebase services. In this section, we'll explore serverless architecture with Firebase and discuss its benefits.

Key Concepts of Serverless Architecture

Serverless architecture is built on several fundamental principles:

1. **No Server Management**: In a serverless architecture, you don't need to provision, manage, or scale servers. The cloud provider takes care of server infrastructure, including scaling up or down based on demand.

2. **Event-Driven**: Serverless applications are event-driven. Functions are triggered by specific events, such as HTTP requests, database changes, or scheduled tasks. This event-driven model allows for flexibility and efficiency in resource allocation.

3. **Pay-as-You-Go**: With serverless, you only pay for the resources consumed during function execution. There's no cost for idle or unused resources, making it cost-effective for small to large-scale applications.

4. **Auto-Scaling**: Serverless platforms automatically scale functions to handle varying workloads. This means your application can handle increased traffic without manual intervention.

Benefits of Serverless Architecture with Firebase

Firebase's implementation of serverless architecture offers several advantages:

1. **Scalability**: Firebase Functions auto-scale based on demand. Whether your application experiences a sudden surge in users or remains idle, Firebase handles resource provisioning to maintain performance.

2. **Reduced Complexity**: Developers can focus on writing code that responds to events, rather than managing server infrastructure. This reduces operational overhead and allows for faster development.

3. **Cost Efficiency**: With Firebase Functions, you only pay for the compute resources consumed during function execution. This pay-as-you-go model is cost-effective, especially for applications with varying workloads.

4. **Integration**: Firebase Functions seamlessly integrate with other Firebase services like Firestore, Realtime Database, and Authentication. This tight integration simplifies building real-time and interactive applications.

5. **Third-Party Services**: Firebase Functions can also integrate with third-party services and APIs, allowing you to extend your application's capabilities further.

6. **Security**: Firebase provides security rules and authentication mechanisms to secure your functions and data. You can control access and permissions at a granular level.

Use Cases for Serverless with Firebase

Serverless architecture with Firebase is suitable for various use cases, including:

- **Real-time Applications**: Build real-time chat applications, live dashboards, or collaborative tools with Firebase Realtime Database and serverless functions.

- **Data Processing**: Process and analyze data in real-time as it flows into Firebase Firestore or Realtime Database.

- **Authentication Flows**: Implement custom authentication logic and user management workflows.

- **Notifications**: Send push notifications, emails, or SMS to users based on specific events or triggers.

- **Background Jobs**: Perform background tasks like data cleanup, image processing, or sending scheduled reports.

- **APIs and Microservices**: Create APIs or microservices that can be easily maintained and scaled independently.

Firebase Functions simplify serverless development, allowing developers to create powerful applications with minimal operational overhead. In the next section, we'll explore how to integrate third-party services with Firebase Functions to enhance the functionality of your applications.

Section 7.4: Integrating Third-Party Services

Firebase Functions offer great flexibility when it comes to integrating third-party services into your application. This capability allows you to extend your app's functionality and leverage external services to enhance user experiences. In this section, we will explore how to integrate third-party services with Firebase Functions.

Why Integrate Third-Party Services?

Integrating third-party services can provide numerous benefits, including:

1. **Access to Specialized Features**: Third-party services often offer specialized features or capabilities that can enhance your application. For example, you can integrate a payment gateway for online transactions or a machine learning API for advanced analysis.

2. **Time and Cost Savings**: Rather than building everything from scratch, integrating third-party services can save you time and development costs. You can leverage existing solutions for various functionalities.

3. **Scalability**: Many third-party services are designed to handle high loads and provide scalable solutions. This ensures your application can grow without worrying about infrastructure limitations.

4. **Expertise**: Third-party providers are often experts in their respective domains. By integrating their services, you benefit from their knowledge and expertise, ensuring the quality of the integrated features.

Steps to Integrate Third-Party Services with Firebase Functions

Integrating third-party services with Firebase Functions typically involves the following steps:

1. **Select the Service**: Choose the third-party service that meets your application's requirements. This could be a service for payments, geolocation, data analysis, or any other functionality.

2. **Set Up Credentials**: Most third-party services require authentication credentials, such as API keys or access tokens. Ensure you have the necessary credentials to interact with the service.

3. **Write the Function**: Create a Firebase Function that uses the third-party service's SDK or API to perform the desired functionality. This can involve making API requests, handling responses, and processing data.

4. **Security**: Implement security measures to protect sensitive data and credentials. Firebase provides security rules and environment variables to securely store sensitive information.

5. **Testing**: Thoroughly test your Firebase Function to ensure it integrates correctly
    with the third-party service. Test various scenarios, including success and error
    cases.

6. **Deployment**: Deploy the Firebase Function to make it available for your
    application. Use the Firebase CLI to deploy the function to the cloud.

Let's consider an example of integrating the Stripe payment gateway with Firebase
Functions for processing payments in an e-commerce application.

```javascript
const functions = require('firebase-functions');
const stripe = require('stripe')(functions.config().stripe.secret_key);

exports.createStripePayment = functions.https.onRequest(async (req, res) => {
  try {
    const { amount, currency, description, source } = req.body;

    // Create a payment charge using the Stripe API
    const paymentIntent = await stripe.paymentIntents.create({
      amount,
      currency,
      description,
      source,
    });

    // Return the payment intent to the client
    res.json({ paymentIntent });
  } catch (error) {
    res.status(500).json({ error: error.message });
  }
});
```

In this example, we integrate Stripe for processing payments. The Firebase Function
createStripePayment receives payment details as a request and uses the Stripe API to
create a payment intent. The response contains the payment intent, which can be used for
further processing or confirmation.

This is just one example of how you can integrate a third-party service with Firebase
Functions. Depending on your application's requirements, you can integrate various
services to add functionalities like geolocation, machine learning, email delivery, and more.

By effectively integrating third-party services with Firebase Functions, you can create
feature-rich and powerful applications without the need to build everything from scratch.
In the next section, we'll explore how to monitor and debug Firebase Functions to ensure
smooth operation.

Section 7.5: Monitoring and Debugging Cloud Functions

Monitoring and debugging are essential aspects of maintaining the reliability and performance of Firebase Functions. In this section, we will delve into the importance of monitoring and debugging Firebase Functions and explore the tools and best practices available for these tasks.

The Importance of Monitoring

Monitoring Firebase Functions is crucial to:

1. **Identify Issues**: It helps you quickly detect and identify any errors or issues that may arise during the execution of functions. Timely detection is vital for minimizing downtime and user impact.

2. **Performance Optimization**: Monitoring provides insights into the performance of your functions. You can identify bottlenecks, slow-performing functions, or resource-intensive operations that need optimization.

3. **Scaling**: As your application grows, monitoring helps you assess the impact of increased usage on function performance. It aids in scaling your functions to handle higher loads.

4. **Resource Management**: Monitoring helps you manage resources effectively. You can monitor resource utilization, such as memory and CPU, to ensure efficient use of cloud resources.

Firebase Functions Logs

Firebase Functions provide a built-in logging system that captures logs generated during function execution. These logs are essential for debugging and monitoring. To log messages within your functions, you can use the `console.log()`, `console.error()`, and `console.warn()` functions.

```javascript
exports.myFunction = functions.https.onRequest((req, res) => {
  console.log('Function execution started');
  // Your function code here
  console.log('Function execution completed');
  res.status(200).send('Function executed successfully');
});
```

Viewing Logs

You can view Firebase Functions logs in several ways:

1. **Firebase Console**: You can access logs through the Firebase console. Go to the Firebase project, navigate to "Functions," and click on the specific function. There, you can view logs in real-time.

2. **Firebase CLI**: Use the Firebase CLI to stream logs to your terminal in real-time. Run the following command:

```
firebase functions:log
```

3. **Google Cloud Logging**: Firebase Functions logs are also available in Google Cloud Logging. You can access advanced features like log exports and filtering in Google Cloud Console.

Debugging Firebase Functions is essential for resolving issues and improving performance. Firebase provides debugging tools that make it easier to identify and fix problems.

1. **Local Emulation**: You can use the Firebase Emulator Suite to test functions locally. It allows you to debug functions in a local development environment before deploying to production.

2. **Error Handling**: Implement proper error handling in your functions. Use try-catch blocks to catch and log errors. This helps in identifying the cause of failures.

```javascript
exports.myFunction = functions.https.onRequest(async (req, res) => {
  try {
    // Your function code here
    res.status(200).send('Function executed successfully');
  } catch (error) {
    console.error('Function error:', error);
    res.status(500).send('Function encountered an error');
  }
});
```

3. **Stack Traces**: When an error occurs, Firebase Functions automatically logs stack traces, making it easier to pinpoint the location of the error in your code.

4. **Debugging in Visual Studio Code**: If you use Visual Studio Code, you can set breakpoints in your function code and use the Firebase Functions extension for debugging.

To effectively monitor and debug Firebase Functions, consider these best practices:

1. **Use Descriptive Logs**: Log meaningful messages that provide context. Include relevant information like function inputs, outputs, and timestamps.

2. **Centralize Logs**: Centralize logs in a single location for easy access and analysis. Consider exporting logs to external services or tools.

3. **Alerting**: Set up alerts and notifications for critical errors or performance issues. Firebase allows you to configure alerts based on log entries.

4. **Regular Monitoring**: Continuously monitor your functions to detect issues early. Regularly review logs and performance metrics.

5. **Performance Profiling**: Use profiling tools to identify performance bottlenecks and optimize resource usage.

By incorporating monitoring and debugging practices into your Firebase Functions development workflow, you can maintain the reliability, efficiency, and performance of your serverless functions, ensuring a smooth user experience. In the next chapter, we will explore Firebase Analytics, a powerful tool for gaining insights into user behavior and app performance.

Section 8.1: Overview of Firebase Analytics

Firebase Analytics is a robust and user-centric app measurement and tracking tool provided by Google Firebase. It enables you to gather detailed insights into user behavior, app usage, and engagement, which are invaluable for making data-driven decisions to improve your app's performance and user experience.

Key Features of Firebase Analytics

Firebase Analytics offers a range of features that make it a powerful tool for app developers and marketers:

1. **Event Tracking**: You can track specific events in your app, such as button clicks, screen views, and in-app purchases. This allows you to understand how users interact with your app.

2. **User Properties**: Firebase Analytics lets you define custom user properties to segment your audience. For example, you can categorize users based on their subscription status or location.

3. **Audiences**: You can create dynamic user segments based on user behavior and properties. This helps in targeting specific user groups with tailored marketing campaigns.

4. **Conversion Tracking**: Track user journeys and measure conversion rates for important actions, such as sign-ups or purchases. This helps you identify areas for improvement in your app's conversion funnel.

5. **Retention Analysis**: Firebase Analytics provides insights into user retention over time. You can see how many users return to your app after their initial visit.

6. **Funnel Analysis**: Analyze user paths through predefined funnels to identify where users drop off or complete specific actions. This is valuable for optimizing user flows.

7. **User Engagement**: Measure user engagement with metrics like session duration, screen views per session, and user engagement over time.

One of the key advantages of Firebase Analytics is its seamless integration with other Firebase services. You can easily combine analytics data with other Firebase features like Cloud Messaging, Remote Config, and A/B Testing to create a holistic app improvement strategy.

To start using Firebase Analytics in your app, follow these steps:

1. **Add Firebase to Your Project**: If you haven't already, add Firebase to your project using the Firebase Console. This step involves creating a Firebase project and configuring your app.

2. **Add the SDK**: Integrate the Firebase Analytics SDK into your app. Depending on your platform (iOS, Android, web), Firebase provides platform-specific instructions for adding the SDK.

3. **Initialize Firebase**: Initialize Firebase Analytics in your app by calling the appropriate initialization method. This usually involves adding initialization code in your app's entry point.

4. **Set Up Events**: Define the events you want to track in your app, such as button clicks, screen views, or custom events. Implement event tracking code in the relevant parts of your app's codebase.

```java
// Example event tracking in an Android app
FirebaseAnalytics.getInstance(context).logEvent("button_click", null);
```

5. **View Analytics Data**: Once you've implemented Firebase Analytics and users interact with your app, you can view the analytics data in the Firebase Console. You can explore user insights, track events, and create custom reports to gain valuable information about your app's performance.

Firebase Analytics provides a wealth of data to help you understand your app's user base, their behaviors, and their preferences. By leveraging these insights, you can make informed decisions to enhance your app and improve user satisfaction. In the next section, we'll dive deeper into event tracking and user behavior analysis with Firebase Analytics.

Section 8.2: Event Tracking and User Behavior Analysis

Event tracking is a fundamental aspect of Firebase Analytics that allows you to gain insights into how users interact with your app. By defining and tracking events, you can understand user behavior, measure the success of specific actions, and make informed decisions to enhance your app's functionality and user experience.

Defining Events

Events are user interactions or important actions within your app that you want to track. Firebase Analytics provides a set of predefined events, such as screen_view and app_open, but you can also define custom events that are specific to your app's functionality. Examples of custom events include button clicks, in-app purchases, or form submissions.

Event Parameters

Events can include parameters to provide additional context and detail about the event. For example, if you're tracking a button click event, you might include parameters like the button's label or the screen where the button was clicked. These parameters help you analyze event data more effectively.

```java
// Example of tracking a button click event with parameters in an Android app
Bundle params = new Bundle();
params.putString("button_label", "checkout_button");
FirebaseAnalytics.getInstance(context).logEvent("button_click", params);
```

Event Reporting

Firebase Analytics offers various ways to report on tracked events:

1. **Event Count**: You can see how many times a specific event has occurred. This metric helps you understand the popularity of certain actions in your app.

2. **Event Parameters**: Analyzing event parameters allows you to segment event data. For instance, you can filter button click events by button label to see which buttons are clicked the most.

3. **Event Duration**: If your events have a time component, you can measure event duration to understand how long users spend on particular actions.

4. **Event Value**: For events that have a quantifiable value, such as in-app purchases, you can track event values to determine the financial impact of specific actions.

User Behavior Analysis

Event tracking enables you to perform user behavior analysis, helping you answer questions like:

- Which features of my app are used the most and the least?
- What user actions lead to conversions, such as sign-ups or purchases?

- Where do users drop off in multi-step processes, like onboarding or checkout?

By segmenting users based on their interactions and behaviors, you can tailor your app's user experience and marketing efforts. Firebase Analytics allows you to create audiences based on event data, making it possible to target specific user groups with personalized content and notifications.

Conversion Funnel Analysis

Another valuable aspect of user behavior analysis is the ability to create and analyze conversion funnels. A conversion funnel is a series of events that lead to a specific goal, such as completing a purchase. Firebase Analytics lets you define and visualize these funnels, helping you identify where users drop off and optimizing the user journey to improve conversion rates.

In summary, event tracking and user behavior analysis are essential components of Firebase Analytics that empower you to understand how users engage with your app. By defining events, tracking parameters, and analyzing user behavior, you can make data-driven decisions to enhance your app's functionality, user experience, and overall success. The next section explores custom metrics and reporting capabilities in Firebase Analytics, providing deeper insights into your app's performance.

Section 8.3: Custom Metrics and Reporting

While Firebase Analytics provides a rich set of predefined events and user properties, there are cases where you need to track specific app metrics that are unique to your application. This is where custom metrics come into play. Firebase allows you to define and track custom metrics, enabling you to gather insights into precisely what matters most to your app's success.

Defining Custom Metrics

To create a custom metric, you need to define it within the Firebase console. Custom metrics can be numeric values representing various aspects of user behavior or app performance. Examples of custom metrics include:

- **High Score**: If you have a game app, you can track the highest score achieved by each player as a custom metric.
- **Session Duration**: Measure how long users typically spend within your app during a session.
- **Conversion Rate**: Calculate the percentage of users who complete a specific goal, such as making a purchase or signing up.

Once you've defined a custom metric, you can log data for that metric using the Firebase Analytics SDK in your app.

Logging custom metric data is straightforward. Here's an example in Android using the Firebase Analytics SDK:

```java
// Log a custom metric value
int highScore = 1000; // Replace with the actual high score value
Bundle params = new Bundle();
params.putInt("high_score", highScore);
FirebaseAnalytics.getInstance(context).logEvent("custom_metric", params);
```

In this example, we're logging the high score as a custom metric called "custom_metric."

Custom Metric Reporting

Firebase Analytics provides various ways to report on custom metrics:

1. **Event-Level Reporting**: You can associate custom metrics with events and analyze them alongside other event data. For example, you can track the high score achieved during a game level completion event.

2. **User-Level Reporting**: Custom metrics can also be used to segment users based on their metric values. This segmentation can help you understand how users with different behaviors contribute to your app's success.

3. **Funnel Analysis**: Custom metrics can be incorporated into conversion funnels, allowing you to analyze how users' metric values impact their journey towards a goal.

4. **Audience Creation**: You can create audiences based on custom metric values. For instance, you can create an audience of users who achieved a high score above a certain threshold and engage them with targeted messaging or rewards.

Custom Metric Best Practices

When working with custom metrics, keep the following best practices in mind:

- Define metrics that align with your app's key performance indicators (KPIs) and goals.
- Avoid creating too many custom metrics, as it can lead to complexity in analysis.
- Ensure consistency in metric naming and data types across your app.

Custom metrics empower you to gain deeper insights into specific aspects of your app's performance and user behavior. By defining, logging, and analyzing custom metrics, you can make informed decisions to optimize your app, enhance user engagement, and achieve your app's objectives.

The next section explores how Firebase Analytics can be integrated with big data tools and platforms, allowing you to leverage the full potential of your app's data for in-depth analysis and insights.

Firebase Analytics provides valuable insights into your app's user behavior and performance, but to gain even deeper insights and leverage the full potential of your app's data, you may want to integrate Firebase Analytics with big data tools and platforms. This integration allows you to perform advanced data analysis, create custom reports, and gain a deeper understanding of your users' interactions with your app.

Firebase Analytics Export

Firebase Analytics offers a feature called "BigQuery Export" that allows you to export your app's analytics data to Google BigQuery, a powerful cloud-based data warehouse. This integration gives you access to raw event data, user properties, and custom dimensions, enabling you to run complex SQL queries, build custom dashboards, and perform advanced analytics.

Setting Up Firebase Analytics Export to BigQuery

1. **Enable BigQuery Export**: In the Firebase console, navigate to your project settings and enable the BigQuery Export feature.

2. **Link BigQuery Project**: Link your Firebase project to a Google Cloud Platform (GCP) project that has BigQuery enabled.

3. **Define Exported Data**: Choose which app events, user properties, and custom dimensions you want to export to BigQuery. You can select specific data to keep your dataset manageable.

4. **Schedule Export**: You can configure how frequently the data is exported to BigQuery. You can choose daily or hourly exports, depending on your needs.

Benefits of BigQuery Integration

Integrating Firebase Analytics with BigQuery offers several advantages:

1. **Raw Data Access**: You gain access to raw, unaggregated event data, allowing you to perform ad-hoc analysis and answer specific questions about user behavior.

2. **Custom Analysis**: You can create custom SQL queries and data transformations to perform advanced analysis tailored to your app's unique requirements.

3. **Custom Reporting**: Build custom dashboards and reports in tools like Google Data Studio, Tableau, or Looker using BigQuery as the data source.

4. **Data Retention**: BigQuery allows you to retain your data for extended periods, giving you historical insights into your app's performance.

Here are some examples of queries you can run in BigQuery after exporting Firebase Analytics data:

Query 1: User Retention

```
SELECT
  event_date AS date,
  COUNT(DISTINCT user_pseudo_id) AS active_users
FROM
  `your-project-id.your-dataset-id.your-table-id`
WHERE
  event_name = 'first_open'
GROUP BY
  date
```

This query calculates the number of active users who opened your app for the first time each day.

Query 2: Funnel Analysis

```
WITH funnel_data AS (
  SELECT
    user_pseudo_id,
    event_name,
    event_timestamp
  FROM
    `your-project-id.your-dataset-id.your-table-id`
  WHERE
    event_name IN ('step_1', 'step_2', 'step_3')
)

SELECT
  event_name,
  COUNT(DISTINCT user_pseudo_id) AS step_count
FROM
  funnel_data
GROUP BY
  event_name
```

This query helps you analyze user progression through a multi-step process within your app.

Security and Compliance

When working with sensitive user data, it's essential to follow best practices for data security and compliance. Ensure that your BigQuery dataset is properly secured and compliant with relevant data protection regulations, such as GDPR.

Integrating Firebase Analytics with BigQuery opens up a world of possibilities for advanced data analysis, custom reporting, and gaining deeper insights into your app's performance.

By leveraging this integration, you can make data-driven decisions to improve user engagement, optimize your app, and drive growth.

Section 8.5: Using Analytics to Drive App Improvements

Firebase Analytics is not just a tool for tracking user behavior and app performance; it's a powerful resource for making data-driven decisions and driving continuous improvements in your mobile or web app. In this section, we'll explore how you can use the insights gathered from Firebase Analytics to enhance your app and provide a better user experience.

Identifying User Behavior Patterns

One of the primary benefits of Firebase Analytics is its ability to help you understand how users interact with your app. By analyzing user behavior patterns, you can identify which features are popular, where users drop off, and which paths lead to conversion. Armed with this information, you can make informed decisions about optimizing your app's user interface and functionality.

A/B Testing and Experimentation

Firebase A/B Testing allows you to create experiments to test different variations of your app's features or UI elements. You can use analytics data to target specific user segments and measure the impact of changes on key metrics such as retention, conversion rate, or revenue. This iterative approach enables you to refine your app based on data-driven insights.

Event Tracking for Key Actions

Event tracking is a fundamental aspect of Firebase Analytics. By defining custom events that align with your app's goals, you can monitor and analyze how users engage with specific actions. For example, you can track events such as "completed purchase," "signed up," or "shared content." These events provide valuable data on user conversions and help you understand the effectiveness of your app's features.

Setting Conversion Goals

Firebase Analytics allows you to set conversion goals, which are specific actions or events you want users to complete in your app. By defining these goals, you can track the conversion rate and identify potential bottlenecks in the user journey. For instance, if you have an e-commerce app, your conversion goal might be the completion of a purchase. Analyzing the conversion funnel can help you pinpoint where users are dropping out of the buying process and take steps to improve it.

User Segmentation

Segmenting your user base is essential for delivering personalized experiences and targeted messaging. Firebase Analytics enables you to create user segments based on various criteria, such as demographics, user properties, or user behavior. By segmenting users, you can tailor your marketing efforts, notifications, and in-app experiences to specific groups, increasing engagement and retention.

Data-Driven Decision Making

The key to leveraging Firebase Analytics effectively is to adopt a data-driven decision-making process. Regularly review your analytics data, identify trends, and use this information to prioritize app improvements. Whether you're optimizing the onboarding experience, refining user flows, or tweaking in-app content, let the data guide your decisions.

Iterative App Improvement

Improving your app is an ongoing process. Firebase Analytics provides you with the tools and insights needed to iterate and evolve your app continuously. As you make changes and enhancements based on analytics data, remember to monitor the impact of these changes and iterate further to achieve your app's goals.

Conclusion

Firebase Analytics is a valuable asset for any app developer or marketer. It empowers you to understand user behavior, track key metrics, and make data-backed decisions to enhance your app's user experience and drive success. By harnessing the power of Firebase Analytics, you can continuously improve your app, increase user engagement, and achieve your business objectives.

Chapter 9: Firebase Performance Monitoring

Section 9.1: Understanding Performance Monitoring

Firebase Performance Monitoring is a powerful tool that allows developers to gain insights into their app's performance and user experience. It provides real-time data on various aspects of your app's performance, helping you identify and address performance bottlenecks, crashes, and issues that may affect user satisfaction. In this section, we will delve into the fundamentals of Firebase Performance Monitoring and how it can benefit your app development process.

What Is Firebase Performance Monitoring?

Firebase Performance Monitoring is a part of the Firebase suite of tools that focuses on monitoring your app's performance and providing actionable insights. It enables you to track the performance of various aspects of your app, including:

1. **App Start Time:** Measure the time it takes for your app to launch and become usable on a user's device.

2. **Screen Rendering:** Analyze how long it takes to render screens and ensure smooth transitions between different views.

3. **Network Requests:** Track the time taken for network requests to complete, helping you identify slow APIs or servers.

4. **Crash Reporting:** Gain visibility into app crashes and errors, allowing you to fix issues quickly.

5. **Custom Traces:** Define custom performance traces for specific actions or events within your app to monitor their execution time.

Key Features and Benefits

Firebase Performance Monitoring offers several key features and benefits:

- **Real-Time Monitoring:** Get real-time data on your app's performance, allowing you to react promptly to any performance degradation.

- **Custom Metrics:** Define custom performance metrics that are relevant to your app's specific use cases, giving you tailored insights.

- **Error Tracking:** Identify and diagnose crashes and errors that can impact the user experience.

- **Performance Alerts:** Set up alerts to receive notifications when performance thresholds are breached, ensuring proactive issue resolution.

- **Integration with Other Firebase Services:** Firebase Performance Monitoring seamlessly integrates with other Firebase services, making it a valuable addition to your Firebase-powered app.

How It Works

Firebase Performance Monitoring works by instrumenting your app's code to collect performance data during runtime. It records key performance metrics, such as response times, and aggregates this data in the Firebase console for analysis. You can then visualize this data in various forms, such as charts and graphs, to gain insights into your app's performance.

Use Cases

Firebase Performance Monitoring is beneficial in various scenarios:

- **Optimizing App Load Time:** Understand the factors contributing to your app's load time and optimize it for a better user experience.

- **Identifying Slow Screens:** Pinpoint screens that take too long to render and work on improving their performance.

- **Monitoring Third-Party Services:** Keep an eye on the performance of third-party services your app relies on, ensuring they meet your expectations.

- **Proactive Issue Resolution:** Receive alerts and notifications for critical performance issues, allowing you to address them before they impact users significantly.

Getting Started

To start using Firebase Performance Monitoring, you need to integrate the Firebase SDK into your app. Once integrated, you can set up custom traces, monitor app performance, and configure alerts through the Firebase console.

In the following sections, we will explore how to set up and configure Firebase Performance Monitoring and how to leverage its features to improve your app's performance and user experience.

Section 9.2: Setting Up and Configuring Performance Monitoring

Once you've decided to integrate Firebase Performance Monitoring into your app, the next step is setting it up and configuring it to collect the necessary performance data. In this section, we'll walk you through the process of getting Firebase Performance Monitoring up and running in your app.

Before you begin, make sure you have the following prerequisites in place:

1. **Firebase Project:** You should have an existing Firebase project where you want to integrate Performance Monitoring.

2. **Firebase SDK:** Ensure that you've integrated the Firebase SDK into your app. If you haven't, follow the Firebase documentation to do so.

Enabling Performance Monitoring

To enable Performance Monitoring, follow these steps:

1. **Firebase Console:** Go to the Firebase Console (https://console.firebase.google.com/), select your project, and navigate to the "Performance" section in the left sidebar.

2. **Enable Performance Monitoring:** Click on "Performance" and then click the "Get started" button to enable Performance Monitoring for your project.

3. **Add SDK Dependency:** In your app-level build.gradle file, add the Firebase Performance Monitoring SDK as a dependency:

```
implementation 'com.google.firebase:firebase-perf:latest_version'
```

Be sure to replace `latest_version` with the current version of the Firebase Performance Monitoring SDK.

4. **Initialize Firebase:** In your app's code, initialize Firebase as early as possible. You typically do this in your app's `Application` class or the main activity's `onCreate` method:

```java
import com.google.firebase.FirebaseApp;

public class MyApp extends Application {
    @Override
    public void onCreate() {
        super.onCreate();
        FirebaseApp.initializeApp(this);
    }
}
```

Make sure you replace `"MyApp"` with the name of your application class.

5. **Configure Performance Monitoring:** In your app's code, you can configure Performance Monitoring by setting various options. For example, you can set the network request sampling rate:

```java
import com.google.firebase.perf.FirebasePerformance;
import com.google.firebase.perf.metrics.Trace;
```

```java
// Set the network request sampling rate to 10%.
FirebasePerformance.getInstance().setPerformanceCollectionEnabled(true)
;
FirebasePerformance.getInstance().setPerformanceCollectionEnabledForTes
ting(true);
```

This code enables performance data collection and sets a custom sampling rate.

Performance Monitoring allows you to define custom traces to measure specific parts of your app's code. These custom traces provide granular insights into the performance of critical functions or actions within your app.

Here's an example of how to create and use a custom trace:

```java
import com.google.firebase.perf.FirebasePerformance;
import com.google.firebase.perf.metrics.Trace;

// Create a custom trace for a specific operation.
Trace customTrace = FirebasePerformance.getInstance().newTrace("custom_trace"
);

// Start the trace when the operation begins.
customTrace.start();

// Perform the operation you want to measure.

// End the trace when the operation is complete.
customTrace.stop();
```

Custom traces allow you to measure the execution time of specific code blocks and gain insights into their performance.

Once Performance Monitoring is enabled and configured, you can view performance data in the Firebase Console. The console provides detailed insights into various aspects of your app's performance, including response times, network requests, and custom traces.

In the next section, we'll explore how to analyze and interpret performance data collected by Firebase Performance Monitoring, helping you make informed decisions to optimize your app's performance and user experience.

Section 9.3: Analyzing App Performance Data

After setting up and configuring Firebase Performance Monitoring, the next crucial step is analyzing the performance data collected by the tool. In this section, we will delve into the process of analyzing this data to gain valuable insights into your app's performance and identify areas that require improvement.

Firebase Performance Dashboard

The Firebase Console provides a dedicated Performance dashboard where you can access detailed performance data and visualizations for your app. To access the dashboard, follow these steps:

1. **Firebase Console:** Go to the Firebase Console (https://console.firebase.google.com/), select your project, and navigate to the "Performance" section in the left sidebar.

2. **Performance Dashboard:** Click on "Performance" to access the Performance dashboard.

Key Performance Metrics

The Performance dashboard offers a variety of key performance metrics that provide insights into different aspects of your app's performance. Here are some essential metrics to monitor:

1. Trace Metrics:

- **Response Time:** Measures the time it takes for various operations in your app to complete.
- **Network Request Time:** Tracks the duration of network requests made by your app.
- **Custom Traces:** Allows you to measure the execution time of specific custom traces.

2. Network Metrics:

- **Network Requests:** Displays detailed information about network requests, including response times and success rates.
- **Network Errors:** Highlights errors and issues related to network requests.

3. App Version Comparison:

- **Compare Versions:** You can compare the performance of different app versions to identify improvements or regressions.

4. Performance Insights:

- **Issues:** The dashboard may highlight performance issues detected in your app, helping you prioritize areas for improvement.

When analyzing performance data, it's essential to look for trends and patterns. Here are some tips for effective analysis:

1. *Identify Performance Bottlenecks: Look for traces or network requests with significantly higher response times or error rates. These may indicate performance bottlenecks that need attention.*

2. *Compare Versions: Use the "App Version Comparison" feature to compare the performance of different app versions. This can help you track improvements or regressions over time.*

3. *Custom Traces: Analyze custom traces to gain insights into specific parts of your app's code. Look for areas where custom traces show higher execution times.*

4. *Network Insights: Examine network metrics to identify slow or failed network requests. This information is crucial for ensuring a smooth user experience, especially in apps that rely heavily on network communication.*

Performance Alerts

Firebase Performance Monitoring allows you to set up performance alerts to proactively monitor your app's performance. These alerts can notify you when certain performance thresholds are breached, enabling you to take immediate action to resolve issues.

To set up performance alerts, navigate to the "Alerts" section in the Performance dashboard and configure alert conditions based on your app's specific requirements.

Continuous Optimization

App performance optimization is an ongoing process. Regularly monitor performance data, analyze trends, and make necessary improvements to enhance your app's user experience continually. Firebase Performance Monitoring provides the insights and tools needed to make data-driven decisions and deliver a high-quality app to your users.

In the next section, we'll explore how to identify and resolve performance issues in your app using Firebase Performance Monitoring.

Section 9.4: Identifying and Resolving Performance Issues

Identifying and resolving performance issues in your app is a crucial aspect of delivering a smooth and responsive user experience. Firebase Performance Monitoring provides valuable insights and tools to help you pinpoint and address these issues effectively.

Before addressing performance issues, it's essential to analyze the data collected by Firebase Performance Monitoring thoroughly. Look for patterns, trends, and anomalies that can help you identify areas of concern. Here are steps to guide your analysis:

1. **Review Key Metrics:** Start by reviewing key performance metrics, such as response times, network request durations, and custom trace data. Identify traces or requests with unusually high latencies or error rates.

2. **Compare Versions:** Utilize the "App Version Comparison" feature to compare the performance of different app versions. Determine if recent updates have impacted performance positively or negatively.

3. **Custom Traces:** Examine custom trace data to gain insights into specific areas of your app's code. Pay attention to custom traces with extended execution times, as they may indicate performance bottlenecks.

4. **Network Insights:** Investigate network metrics to identify slow or failed network requests. Network-related performance issues can significantly impact user experience, especially in apps with extensive network communication.

Setting Performance Alerts

Firebase Performance Monitoring allows you to set up performance alerts that notify you when specific performance thresholds are breached. These alerts enable you to take immediate action when critical issues arise. Here's how to set up performance alerts:

1. **Access Alerts:** In the Firebase Console, navigate to the "Alerts" section within the Performance dashboard.

2. **Create Alert Conditions:** Define alert conditions based on your app's requirements. You can set thresholds for various metrics, such as response time and error rate.

3. **Notification Channels:** Configure notification channels to receive alerts through various means, such as email, SMS, or webhooks.

4. **Response Plan:** Develop a response plan that outlines the actions to take when an alert is triggered. This ensures a proactive approach to resolving performance issues.

Resolving Performance Bottlenecks

Once you've identified performance bottlenecks, it's time to address them. Here are common strategies for resolving performance issues in your app:

1. **Code Optimization:** Review and optimize the code responsible for slow traces or network requests. Identify and refactor inefficient code paths to improve execution times.

2. **Caching:** Implement caching mechanisms to reduce the need for repetitive network requests. Cached data can be served quickly, improving response times.

3. **Asynchronous Operations:** Make use of asynchronous programming techniques to prevent blocking the main thread and ensure smooth app responsiveness.

4. **Content Delivery Networks (CDNs):** Consider using CDNs to serve static assets and resources, reducing server load and improving content delivery speed.

5. **Database Indexing:** Optimize database queries by creating appropriate indexes. Well-structured queries can significantly reduce database query times.

6. **Network Optimization:** Minimize network payload size, use efficient data formats (e.g., JSON over XML), and implement strategies like data compression to improve network performance.

7. **Testing and Monitoring:** Continuously test and monitor your app's performance after implementing changes. Ensure that optimizations have the desired effect and do not introduce new issues.

Performance Improvement Iteration

App performance optimization is an iterative process. After addressing initial performance issues, continue to monitor your app's performance, analyze data, and make improvements. Regularly revisit performance alerts and adjust alert thresholds as needed to stay proactive in identifying emerging issues.

By following these steps and leveraging Firebase Performance Monitoring, you can maintain a high-performance app that provides an exceptional user experience. In the next section, we'll explore best practices for maintaining consistent high performance throughout your app's lifecycle.

Section 9.5: Best Practices for Maintaining High Performance

Maintaining high performance in your Firebase-powered app is an ongoing effort that requires attention to detail and proactive monitoring. In this section, we'll explore best practices and strategies to ensure your app continues to deliver an excellent user experience throughout its lifecycle.

1. Regularly Review Performance Data

Consistently reviewing performance data collected by Firebase Performance Monitoring is crucial. Set aside time for regular performance analysis to identify any emerging issues or changes in your app's behavior. This practice allows you to address problems promptly and maintain a responsive app.

2. Implement Continuous Integration and Delivery (CI/CD)

Incorporate CI/CD pipelines into your development workflow. Automated testing and deployment processes help catch performance regressions early in the development cycle. This ensures that performance improvements and optimizations are consistently applied to your app.

3. Monitor Third-Party Integrations

If your app relies on third-party services or APIs, closely monitor their performance and availability. Slow or unreliable third-party integrations can negatively impact your app's performance, so have contingency plans in place or consider alternatives if issues persist.

4. Keep Libraries and SDKs Up to Date

Regularly update the libraries, SDKs, and dependencies used in your app, including Firebase SDKs. Newer versions often include performance enhancements and bug fixes. Staying up to date ensures that your app benefits from the latest improvements.

5. Optimize Images and Media

Efficiently manage images and media assets to reduce their impact on performance. Use image compression, lazy loading, and responsive images to minimize load times while maintaining visual quality. Consider using Content Delivery Networks (CDNs) for media delivery.

6. Minimize Network Requests

Every network request adds latency to your app. Minimize unnecessary network requests, combine multiple requests when possible, and use efficient data formats like JSON to reduce payload sizes. Implement caching to store frequently accessed data locally.

7. Load Content Asynchronously

Loading content asynchronously prevents the main thread from blocking, ensuring a responsive user interface. Use techniques like background threads, web workers (for web apps), and asynchronous APIs to handle time-consuming tasks without affecting user interactions.

8. Use Code Splitting

For web applications, consider implementing code splitting techniques to load only the necessary JavaScript code for a particular page or feature. This reduces the initial load time and improves perceived performance.

9. Prioritize Critical Rendering Path

Ensure that your app's critical resources, such as HTML, CSS, and JavaScript, are prioritized to render quickly. Minimize render-blocking resources and use techniques like lazy loading for non-critical elements.

10. Conduct Load Testing

Perform load testing to assess how your app handles heavy traffic and concurrent users. Identify performance bottlenecks under stress conditions and optimize your infrastructure accordingly.

11. A/B Testing for Performance

Leverage A/B testing to compare different app configurations or optimizations and their impact on performance. This data-driven approach allows you to make informed decisions about which improvements to implement.

12. Educate Your Team

Ensure that your development team is well-informed about performance best practices. Conduct training sessions and promote a performance-focused mindset within your organization.

13. User Feedback

Pay attention to user feedback related to performance. Act on user-reported issues promptly and use their input to prioritize performance improvements.

14. Set Performance Goals

Define specific performance goals for your app, such as response time targets or error rate thresholds. Regularly track your progress toward these goals and adjust your optimization efforts accordingly.

By incorporating these best practices into your app development and maintenance processes, you can sustain high performance and provide an exceptional user experience. Remember that performance optimization is an ongoing commitment, and continuous monitoring and improvement are key to long-term success.

Chapter 10: Firebase Test Lab

Section 10.1: Introduction to Firebase Test Lab

Firebase Test Lab is a robust and scalable mobile app testing platform provided by Google. It enables developers to test their Android and iOS apps on a wide range of devices and configurations, helping ensure app quality and reliability. In this section, we'll delve into the fundamentals of Firebase Test Lab, its features, and how to get started with mobile app testing.

What is Firebase Test Lab?

Firebase Test Lab, also known as Google Cloud Test Lab, is a cloud-based testing infrastructure for mobile apps. It allows developers to automate testing on real physical devices and virtual emulators to identify issues, bugs, and performance bottlenecks before releasing their apps to users.

Key Features of Firebase Test Lab:

1. **Device Testing**: Firebase Test Lab offers a vast library of physical Android and iOS devices, covering various screen sizes, operating system versions, and hardware configurations.

2. **Robust Testing Suite**: Developers can create test scenarios using Espresso (for Android) and XCTest (for iOS) to simulate user interactions and validate app functionality.

3. **Test on Real Devices**: Firebase Test Lab executes tests on real, non-rooted devices, providing realistic testing conditions.

4. **Test on Emulators**: Virtual device testing is also available for rapid testing and debugging.

5. **Performance Metrics**: Get insights into app performance, including CPU usage, memory, and network activity, helping you optimize your app for various conditions.

6. **Test Across Device Configurations**: Test your app across different device configurations to ensure compatibility and performance consistency.

7. **Cloud Integration**: Firebase Test Lab seamlessly integrates with Firebase projects, making it easy to include testing in your app development pipeline.

Getting Started with Firebase Test Lab:

To start using Firebase Test Lab, follow these general steps:

1. **Set Up Firebase**: If you haven't already, create a Firebase project and add your app to it.

2. **Integrate Firebase Test Lab**: Include Firebase Test Lab in your project by adding the necessary dependencies and configuration files.

3. **Write Test Scripts**: Create test scripts using Espresso (Android) or XCTest (iOS) for your app's features and functionalities.

4. **Run Tests**: Use the Firebase Test Lab command-line tools or Firebase Console to run your tests on the devices and configurations of your choice.

5. **View Test Results**: Review test results, including pass/fail status and performance metrics, to identify issues and areas for improvement.

6. **Iterate and Improve**: Address any identified issues, iterate on your app, and re-run tests to ensure continual improvement.

Benefits of Using Firebase Test Lab:

- **Increased App Quality**: Comprehensive testing on real devices helps identify and fix issues before users encounter them.

- **Compatibility Assurance**: Test across a wide range of devices and configurations to ensure compatibility with your target audience.

- **Time and Cost Savings**: Automated testing on multiple devices reduces the need for manual testing and speeds up the development process.

- **Performance Optimization**: Monitor and improve app performance based on valuable performance metrics.

- **Integration with CI/CD**: Easily integrate Firebase Test Lab into your continuous integration and continuous deployment (CI/CD) pipeline.

Firebase Test Lab empowers developers to deliver high-quality mobile apps with confidence. In the following sections, we'll explore automated testing strategies, configuring and running tests, analyzing test results, and integrating Firebase Test Lab seamlessly into your development workflow.

Section 10.2: Automated Testing Strategies

Automated testing is a critical component of the software development process, and Firebase Test Lab provides a powerful platform for automating tests on a wide range of devices and configurations. In this section, we will explore various automated testing strategies that can help you ensure the quality and reliability of your mobile apps.

1. Unit Testing:

Unit testing involves testing individual units or components of your code in isolation. For Android apps, you can use popular testing frameworks like JUnit and Mockito. For iOS apps, XCTest is commonly used. Firebase Test Lab doesn't directly support unit testing, but you can run unit tests on your local development environment.

2. Integration Testing:

Integration testing checks how different components of your app work together. Firebase Test Lab allows you to run integration tests on real devices and emulators. You can write test scripts that simulate user interactions and validate the interactions between various parts of your app.

3. UI Testing:

UI testing, also known as end-to-end testing, focuses on testing your app's user interface. For Android, Firebase Test Lab supports Espresso, a popular UI testing framework. For iOS, XCTest can be used for UI testing. You can automate UI tests to ensure that your app's interface behaves correctly on different devices and screen sizes.

4. Performance Testing:

Performance testing is essential to identify bottlenecks and optimize your app's speed and resource usage. Firebase Test Lab provides performance metrics, such as CPU usage, memory consumption, and network activity, to help you measure and improve your app's performance.

5. Compatibility Testing:

Testing your app on a variety of devices and OS versions is crucial to ensure compatibility. Firebase Test Lab offers an extensive catalog of physical devices and emulators, allowing you to test your app on different configurations easily.

6. Continuous Integration (CI) and Continuous Deployment (CD) Testing:

Integrating Firebase Test Lab into your CI/CD pipeline ensures that your app is automatically tested whenever there is a code change or a new build. This helps catch issues early and ensures that only high-quality builds are deployed.

7. A/B Testing:

While Firebase Test Lab primarily focuses on functional and performance testing, you can also use Firebase Remote Config to perform A/B testing. It allows you to test different app configurations and features on a subset of your users to determine which version performs better.

8. Test Automation Frameworks:

To streamline testing, consider using test automation frameworks like Appium, Calabash, or Detox, which are compatible with Firebase Test Lab. These frameworks allow you to write tests that can run on both Android and iOS, reducing testing effort.

9. Test Reporting and Analysis:

Firebase Test Lab provides detailed test reports and logs, making it easy to identify issues. You can analyze test results to pinpoint areas that need improvement and track the progress of your app's testing efforts over time.

Incorporating a combination of these testing strategies into your app development process can significantly enhance the quality and reliability of your mobile applications. Firebase Test Lab's flexibility and scalability make it a valuable tool for automating tests and ensuring that your app performs well on a wide range of devices and configurations.

Section 10.3: Configuring and Running Tests

Configuring and running tests in Firebase Test Lab is a crucial step in ensuring the quality and reliability of your mobile apps. In this section, we'll explore the process of setting up and executing tests using Firebase Test Lab.

1. Firebase Console:

The Firebase Console is the primary interface for configuring and managing tests in Firebase Test Lab. To get started, log in to the Firebase Console and select your project. Then, navigate to the "Test Lab" section.

2. Test Configuration:

Before running tests, you need to define a test configuration. A test configuration specifies the test type (e.g., Robo test, instrumentation test), the test app APK, the device or emulator configuration, and any test parameters.

3. Test Types:

Firebase Test Lab supports various test types, including:

- **Robo Test**: Robo tests are automated tests where Firebase Test Lab explores your app like a real user. It generates random UI events to interact with your app and identify crashes or issues.

- **Instrumentation Test**: Instrumentation tests are written by you to validate specific features of your app. You can use popular testing frameworks like Espresso (Android) or XCTest (iOS) for these tests.

- **Game Loop Test**: Game Loop tests are designed for games and simulate continuous gameplay. They help identify performance and stability issues in gaming apps.

4. Uploading Test APKs:

You need to upload the APK files for your app and test to Firebase Test Lab. Ensure that you have the correct versions of both the app and test APKs.

5. Device Selection:

Firebase Test Lab provides a wide range of physical devices and emulators for testing. You can choose specific devices and configurations or opt for a "Robo test" that runs on a random selection of devices.

6. Test Parameters:

Depending on the test type, you may need to specify additional parameters, such as test timeout, orientation, and locale settings. These parameters help customize the testing environment.

7. Running Tests:

Once your test configuration is set up, you can initiate test runs from the Firebase Console. Firebase Test Lab will execute the tests on the selected devices and generate detailed reports.

8. Test Results:

After the tests are completed, Firebase Test Lab provides comprehensive test reports that include information about test outcomes, device logs, screenshots, videos, and performance data. You can access these reports from the Firebase Console.

9. Continuous Integration (CI) Integration:

To automate testing as part of your development workflow, integrate Firebase Test Lab with your CI/CD pipeline. Popular CI/CD platforms like Jenkins, CircleCI, and Travis CI can trigger test runs in Firebase Test Lab upon code changes or new builds.

10. Monitoring and Alerts:

Firebase Test Lab allows you to set up monitoring and alerts to be notified of test failures or performance regressions. You can configure alerting rules based on specific criteria to ensure timely detection of issues.

11. Test History:

Firebase Test Lab maintains a history of test runs, making it easy to track the progress of your app's testing efforts over time. You can compare test results from different runs to identify improvements or regressions.

By effectively configuring and running tests in Firebase Test Lab, you can identify and address issues in your mobile apps early in the development process. This leads to higher-quality apps and improved user experiences.

Section 10.4: Analyzing Test Results

Analyzing test results is a critical aspect of the testing process in Firebase Test Lab. It provides valuable insights into the performance and quality of your mobile app. In this section, we will explore how to interpret and utilize test results effectively.

1. Test Reports:

Firebase Test Lab generates comprehensive test reports for each test run. These reports include detailed information about the test, such as the test configuration, device details, test outcomes, and any issues encountered during testing.

2. Test Outcomes:

Test outcomes are categorized into several statuses, including:

- **Passed**: The test ran successfully without any issues.
- **Failed**: The test encountered one or more failures, such as crashes, ANRs (Application Not Responding), or assertion failures.
- **Skipped**: Some tests may be skipped due to various reasons, such as incompatible device configurations.
- **Timed Out**: Tests that exceed the specified time limit are marked as timed out.

3. Device Logs:

Firebase Test Lab captures device logs during test execution. These logs can be invaluable for diagnosing issues, as they provide insights into the behavior of your app during testing. You can view and download these logs from the test report.

4. Screenshots and Videos:

For UI tests, Firebase Test Lab captures screenshots and videos of the test scenarios. This visual data helps in identifying user interface issues, layout problems, or unexpected behavior. You can access these assets within the test report.

5. Performance Metrics:

Firebase Test Lab provides detailed performance metrics, including CPU usage, memory usage, network usage, and battery consumption. These metrics help you understand how your app performs on different devices and configurations.

6. Crash Reports:

In case of test failures due to app crashes, Firebase Test Lab generates crash reports. These reports include stack traces and information about the device and Android version where the crash occurred. For iOS apps, similar crash information is provided.

7. Performance Regression:

By comparing the performance metrics across different test runs, you can identify performance regressions. This is crucial for ensuring that app updates do not degrade performance on specific devices or scenarios.

8. Debugging and Issue Resolution:

When tests fail, you can use the collected data, including device logs, screenshots, and crash reports, to debug and resolve issues. Firebase Test Lab provides a rich set of resources to aid in the debugging process.

9. Continuous Integration:

Integrate test result analysis into your CI/CD pipeline. Automated analysis of test results can trigger alerts and actions based on specific criteria, ensuring that issues are addressed promptly.

10. Test Report Sharing:

Share test reports with your team or stakeholders directly from the Firebase Console. Collaboration is made easier when team members can access and review test results.

11. Iterative Testing:

Firebase Test Lab supports iterative testing, allowing you to make changes to your app based on the feedback and issues identified in test reports. After addressing issues, rerun tests to ensure improvements.

12. Version Control:

Consider version control for test configurations and test results. Storing test configurations in version control systems like Git enables you to track changes and collaborate on test setups.

Analyzing test results in Firebase Test Lab is an iterative process. It involves a continuous feedback loop where you identify issues, resolve them, and iteratively improve the quality and performance of your mobile app. Utilize the insights gained from test reports to create a robust and reliable application for your users.

Section 10.5: Continuous Integration and Delivery with Firebase

Continuous Integration (CI) and Continuous Delivery (CD) are integral to modern software development practices. They enable teams to automate the building, testing, and deployment of applications, ensuring that software can be released reliably and frequently. Firebase provides tools and integrations that streamline the CI/CD pipeline for mobile and web apps. In this section, we will explore how to set up CI/CD workflows using Firebase.

1. Firebase CLI:

The Firebase Command Line Interface (CLI) is a crucial tool for setting up CI/CD workflows. You can use the CLI to interact with various Firebase services, including hosting, Firestore, and Cloud Functions, in an automated manner.

2. Cloud Build Integration:

Firebase can be integrated with Google Cloud Build, a CI/CD platform that automates build, test, and deployment processes. You can configure Google Cloud Build to trigger Firebase actions, such as deploying to Firebase Hosting or running tests in Firebase Test Lab, whenever changes are pushed to your version control repository.

3. GitHub Actions:

If your codebase is hosted on GitHub, you can leverage GitHub Actions to automate Firebase workflows. Create workflows that deploy to Firebase Hosting, run tests, and trigger other Firebase actions whenever code changes are pushed to your GitHub repository.

4. Bitbucket Pipelines:

For Bitbucket users, Bitbucket Pipelines can be used to automate Firebase tasks. Similar to GitHub Actions, you can configure pipelines to build, test, and deploy your app using Firebase services.

5. GitLab CI/CD:

GitLab CI/CD can also be employed to automate Firebase workflows. Define CI/CD pipelines in your GitLab repository to build, test, and deploy your app to Firebase Hosting or other Firebase services.

6. Continuous Testing:

Integrate Firebase Test Lab into your CI/CD pipeline to perform automated testing on different device configurations. Run tests as part of your build process to catch issues early and ensure app quality.

7. Deployment Staging:

Set up staging environments in Firebase Hosting to preview changes before deploying to production. This allows you to test new features or updates with a select group of users or stakeholders.

8. Rollback Strategies:

Implement rollback strategies in your CI/CD pipeline to quickly revert to a previous version of your app in case of issues or unexpected behavior in the production environment.

9. Monitoring and Alerts:

Integrate Firebase Performance Monitoring and Firebase Crashlytics into your CI/CD pipeline to monitor app performance and detect crashes in real-time. Set up alerts to be notified of critical issues immediately.

10. Gradual Rollouts:

Utilize Firebase Remote Config and Firebase Hosting's versioning to perform gradual rollouts of new features or updates. Monitor user engagement and app performance during these rollouts.

11. Environment Variables:

Securely manage environment-specific configurations and secrets using Firebase Hosting's environment variables feature. This ensures that sensitive data is not exposed in your code repository.

12. Documentation and Versioning:

Maintain clear documentation for your CI/CD pipeline setup, including instructions for team members on how to use and configure CI/CD workflows. Consider versioning your CI/CD configurations to track changes over time.

By integrating Firebase with your CI/CD pipeline, you can automate repetitive tasks, increase development velocity, and ensure the reliability and quality of your applications. Continuous testing, deployment staging, and monitoring are essential components of a robust CI/CD workflow that empowers your team to deliver software efficiently and with confidence.

Chapter 11: Firebase Predictions

Section 11.1: Leveraging Machine Learning in Firebase

Firebase Predictions is a powerful feature that allows developers to harness the capabilities of machine learning to improve user engagement and app performance. Machine learning has become an integral part of modern app development, and Firebase Predictions makes it accessible to developers without requiring extensive knowledge of machine learning algorithms.

Understanding Firebase Predictions

Firebase Predictions uses the power of Google's machine learning algorithms to analyze user data and generate predictions about user behavior. These predictions can help you tailor your app's content and features to individual users, increasing user engagement and retention.

Setting Up Predictions for User Behavior

To get started with Firebase Predictions, you need to integrate Firebase into your app and enable Predictions in the Firebase console. Once enabled, Firebase will start collecting user data, such as user demographics, engagement metrics, and in-app behavior.

Firebase Predictions leverages this data to create predictive models. These models can anticipate user actions, such as churn prediction (predicting when a user might stop using your app) and user conversion prediction (predicting when a user might make an in-app purchase or subscribe to a service).

Creating Custom Prediction Models

While Firebase Predictions offers pre-built prediction models, you can also create custom prediction models tailored to your app's specific needs. Custom models allow you to define your own prediction goals and use cases.

Creating a custom prediction model involves selecting the desired prediction goal, specifying the user properties and event triggers to consider, and training the model with historical user data.

Integrating Predictions with Firebase Services

One of the strengths of Firebase Predictions is its seamless integration with other Firebase services. You can use Predictions to enhance various aspects of your app, such as sending personalized notifications, optimizing in-app advertising, and recommending content based on user preferences.

For example, you can use Predictions to identify users who are likely to churn and then target them with personalized offers or content to encourage them to stay engaged with your app.

While Firebase Predictions offers valuable insights and automation, it's essential to follow best practices to make the most of this feature. Some best practices include:

1. **Data Quality**: Ensure that your user data is accurate and up-to-date to improve the accuracy of predictions.

2. **Monitor Predictions**: Regularly monitor the performance of your predictions and adjust your strategies based on the results.

3. **User Privacy**: Respect user privacy and comply with data protection regulations when collecting and using user data for predictions.

4. **Experimentation**: Use A/B testing and experimentation to validate the effectiveness of your prediction-driven strategies.

In conclusion, Firebase Predictions is a valuable tool for app developers looking to leverage machine learning to enhance user engagement and app performance. By understanding user behavior and predicting user actions, you can create a more personalized and engaging experience for your app's users.

Section 11.2: Setting Up Predictions for User Behavior

Setting up Firebase Predictions for user behavior requires a few steps to ensure that your app is collecting the necessary data and that Firebase can generate accurate predictions. Let's explore the process of setting up Predictions for your app.

1. Firebase Integration

Before you can start using Firebase Predictions, you need to integrate Firebase into your app. This involves adding Firebase SDK to your project, configuring Firebase services, and initializing Firebase in your app. You can follow Firebase's official documentation for your specific platform (iOS, Android, or web) to complete this step.

2. Enabling Predictions

Once Firebase is integrated into your app, go to the Firebase console and navigate to the Predictions section. Enable Predictions for your project. Firebase will automatically start collecting user data related to demographics, engagement, and in-app behavior.

3. Understanding Prediction Goals

Before you can create predictions, you need to define your prediction goals. Prediction goals are specific behaviors or actions you want to predict. Firebase provides several predefined prediction goals like "churn," "spend," and "engagement," but you can also create custom prediction goals tailored to your app's needs.

For example, if you run an e-commerce app, your prediction goals might include predicting when a user is likely to make a purchase or predicting when they might abandon their shopping cart.

4. Specifying User Properties and Events

To create accurate predictions, you'll need to specify which user properties and events Firebase should consider. User properties can include demographic information, location, and user attributes. Events are specific actions users take in your app, such as signing in, making a purchase, or viewing a product.

You can choose which user properties and events are relevant to your prediction goal. Firebase will use this data to train the predictive model.

5. Training the Model

Firebase Predictions leverages machine learning to create predictive models. After defining your prediction goal and specifying user properties and events, Firebase will start training the model using historical user data.

Training the model involves analyzing past user behavior to identify patterns and trends. The model will learn from this data to make predictions about future user behavior.

6. Evaluating Predictions

Firebase Predictions continuously evaluates its predictions based on new user data. It updates predictions as new data becomes available, ensuring that predictions remain accurate over time.

7. Integrating Predictions into Your App

Once Firebase Predictions generates predictions, you can integrate them into your app's user experience. For example, you can use predictions to send personalized notifications, recommend content, or target specific user groups with tailored offers.

```
// Example of using a churn prediction to send a personalized message
const isLikelyToChurn = // Retrieve churn prediction result for the user
if (isLikelyToChurn) {
  // Send a personalized message to encourage user engagement
  const message = "We miss you! Enjoy a special discount on your next purchase.";
  sendNotificationToUser(userId, message);
}
```

8. Monitoring and Refining

It's important to monitor the effectiveness of predictions in your app. Firebase provides tools and analytics to track how predictions are impacting user engagement, conversion rates, and other key metrics.

Regularly review prediction performance and make adjustments as needed. You can refine your prediction goals, add or remove user properties and events, and experiment with different strategies to improve user engagement and retention.

In summary, setting up Firebase Predictions for user behavior involves integrating Firebase into your app, enabling Predictions, defining prediction goals, specifying user properties and events, training the predictive model, and integrating predictions into your app's user experience. Continuous monitoring and refinement are essential to maximize the benefits of Predictions for your app.

Section 11.3: Creating Custom Prediction Models

Firebase Predictions provides predefined prediction goals to get you started quickly. However, there might be cases where you need to create custom prediction models tailored to your app's unique requirements. Custom prediction models allow you to predict specific user behaviors or events that are not covered by Firebase's default goals. In this section, we'll explore the process of creating custom prediction models.

1. Identifying Custom Prediction Goals

The first step in creating a custom prediction model is to identify the specific user behavior or event you want to predict. This could be any action or outcome that is critical to your app's success, such as predicting when a user is likely to make a high-value purchase, when they might unsubscribe, or when they are most likely to engage with premium content.

2. Collecting Relevant Data

To create an accurate custom prediction model, you'll need historical user data related to the behavior you want to predict. This data should include user attributes, past actions, and any other information that can help the model learn patterns and trends.

For example, if you want to predict high-value purchases, you'll need data on users who have made such purchases in the past, including their characteristics and the actions they took before making the purchase.

3. Defining User Properties and Events

Similar to predefined prediction goals, you'll need to specify which user properties and events Firebase should consider when creating your custom prediction model. These properties and events should be relevant to the behavior you want to predict.

For instance, if you're predicting high-value purchases, relevant properties might include the user's previous purchase history, the products they've viewed, and their demographic information. Relevant events could include adding items to a cart or participating in special promotions.

4. Training the Custom Model

Once you've identified your custom prediction goal, collected relevant data, and defined user properties and events, Firebase will start training the custom prediction model. During this phase, Firebase's machine learning algorithms will analyze the data and learn patterns associated with the behavior you want to predict.

Training may take some time, depending on the complexity of your prediction goal and the amount of historical data available. Firebase will automatically update the model as new data becomes available.

5. Evaluating Custom Predictions

After training, Firebase Predictions will provide predictions based on your custom model. You can evaluate the accuracy and effectiveness of these predictions by comparing them to actual user behavior and outcomes.

6. Integration into Your App

Integrating custom predictions into your app's user experience is similar to integrating predefined predictions. You can use the predictions to personalize user interactions, send targeted notifications, or make tailored content recommendations.

```
// Example of using a custom prediction to recommend content
const isLikelyToEngage = // Retrieve custom prediction result for user engage
ment
if (isLikelyToEngage) {
  // Recommend content to the user based on their predicted engagement
  const recommendedContent = getRecommendedContent(userId);
  displayRecommendedContent(recommendedContent);
}
```

7. Monitoring and Refining

As with predefined predictions, it's crucial to monitor and refine custom predictions over time. Regularly assess the model's performance and make adjustments as needed. You can refine the model by adding more relevant data, modifying the user properties and events considered, or fine-tuning the prediction goal criteria.

In summary, creating custom prediction models with Firebase Predictions involves identifying specific prediction goals, collecting relevant historical data, defining user properties and events, training the custom model, evaluating predictions, integrating predictions into your app, and continuously monitoring and refining the model to improve its accuracy and effectiveness. Custom predictions allow you to address unique user behavior scenarios and enhance user engagement and retention in your app.

Section 11.4: Integrating Predictions with Firebase Services

Integrating Firebase Predictions with other Firebase services can enhance your app's user experience and engagement by allowing you to automate personalized interactions and deliver targeted content. In this section, we'll explore how to integrate Firebase Predictions with various Firebase services.

1. Firebase Cloud Messaging (FCM)

Firebase Cloud Messaging (FCM) allows you to send notifications to your app's users. By integrating Predictions with FCM, you can automatically send notifications that are tailored to each user based on their predicted behavior.

For example, if Firebase Predictions predicts that a user is likely to churn (stop using the app), you can use FCM to send them a targeted notification with a special offer to encourage them to stay engaged.

2. Remote Config

Firebase Remote Config enables you to remotely configure aspects of your app's behavior. You can use Predictions to personalize these configurations based on each user's predicted behavior.

For instance, if Firebase Predictions predicts that a user is interested in sports content, you can use Remote Config to adjust the app's default content view to prioritize sports-related articles.

3. Firebase A/B Testing

Firebase A/B Testing allows you to experiment with different variations of your app to optimize user engagement. You can use Predictions to segment users into different groups based on their predicted behavior and test how different app experiences impact their engagement.

For example, you can create A/B tests that deliver different app layouts to users predicted to be interested in different types of content and measure which layout leads to higher engagement.

4. Realtime Database and Firestore

If you're using Firebase Realtime Database or Firestore to store user data or content, you can use Predictions to personalize the data that users see. For instance, you can filter and prioritize content based on Predictions' predictions.

```
// Example of using Predictions to filter Firestore content
const userPredictions = // Retrieve Predictions for the user
```

```javascript
const filteredContent = filterContentBasedOnPredictions(userPredictions);
displayFilteredContent(filteredContent);
```

5. Analytics and Crashlytics

Firebase Analytics and Firebase Crashlytics can provide valuable insights into user behavior and app performance. You can use Predictions to segment users based on their predicted behavior and analyze how different user segments interact with your app or how certain behaviors correlate with app crashes.

6. Authentication and Realtime User Segmentation

Integrating Firebase Predictions with Firebase Authentication allows you to segment users in real-time based on their predicted behavior. This segmentation can help personalize the user experience, such as showing different onboarding flows or offering incentives to users predicted to take specific actions.

```javascript
// Example of real-time user segmentation based on Predictions
const userPredictions = // Retrieve Predictions for the user
if (userPredictions.isLikelyToPurchase) {
  // Show a special onboarding flow for potential high-value customers
  showHighValueOnboarding();
} else {
  // Show a standard onboarding flow for other users
  showStandardOnboarding();
}
```

7. Monitoring and Continuous Improvement

After integrating Predictions with Firebase services, it's essential to monitor the effectiveness of these integrations. Regularly analyze user engagement and retention metrics to ensure that the personalized experiences generated by Predictions are positively impacting your app's performance.

In summary, integrating Firebase Predictions with Firebase services like FCM, Remote Config, A/B Testing, Realtime Database, Firestore, Analytics, Crashlytics, Authentication, and Realtime User Segmentation can significantly enhance your app's ability to provide personalized and engaging experiences to your users. These integrations allow you to automate actions and deliver content that aligns with each user's predicted behavior, ultimately improving user satisfaction and app retention.

Section 11.5: Best Practices for Effective Predictions

In this section, we'll discuss some best practices for effectively using Firebase Predictions to improve user engagement, retention, and overall app performance. These practices will help you make the most out of Predictions and provide a better user experience.

1. Define Clear Goals

Before you start using Firebase Predictions, it's crucial to define clear goals for what you want to achieve. Understand the specific user behaviors or actions you want to predict and influence. Having well-defined goals will guide you in setting up and configuring Predictions effectively.

2. Collect Relevant Data

Firebase Predictions relies on user data to make accurate predictions. Ensure that you collect and send relevant data to Firebase Analytics and other Firebase services. The more data you have, the better Predictions can perform.

3. Continuously Train Predictions

Predictions improve over time as more user data becomes available. Continuously train your Predictions models by regularly sending data and updates to Firebase. This ensures that Predictions stay accurate and up-to-date.

4. Test Predictions Before Deployment

Before deploying Predictions into your production app, test them thoroughly in a development or staging environment. Validate the accuracy of Predictions and verify that they align with your predefined goals.

5. Monitor and Refine Predictions

After deploying Predictions, monitor their performance using Firebase Analytics and other monitoring tools. Keep an eye on user engagement, retention, and conversion rates to assess the impact of Predictions. If necessary, refine your Predictions models and configurations to optimize results.

6. Use Predictions with Other Firebase Services

Integrate Predictions with other Firebase services like Firebase Cloud Messaging (FCM), Remote Config, A/B Testing, and Realtime Database to deliver personalized experiences. Combining Predictions with these services can lead to more effective user engagement strategies.

7. Personalize Content and Experiences

Leverage Predictions to personalize the content and experiences you offer to users. Tailor the app's interface, recommendations, notifications, and incentives based on Predictions' insights into individual user behavior.

```javascript
// Example of personalizing content based on Predictions
const userPredictions = // Retrieve Predictions for the user
const personalizedContent = generatePersonalizedContent(userPredictions);
displayPersonalizedContent(personalizedContent);
```

When using Predictions, ensure that you respect user privacy and comply with relevant data protection regulations. Be transparent about the data you collect and how you use it. Implement data anonymization and user consent mechanisms when necessary.

9. Collaborate Across Teams

Collaboration between product, marketing, and development teams is essential for successful Predictions implementation. Encourage cross-functional collaboration to define goals, create personalized experiences, and analyze the impact of Predictions on different user segments.

10. Stay Informed About Updates

Firebase is continually evolving, and new features and improvements are regularly introduced. Stay informed about updates to Firebase Predictions and related services to take advantage of the latest enhancements and best practices.

By following these best practices, you can effectively harness the power of Firebase Predictions to enhance user engagement, increase user retention, and drive positive outcomes for your mobile or web application. Predictions, when used thoughtfully and in alignment with your app's goals, can be a valuable tool in delivering personalized and engaging experiences to your users.

Chapter 12: Firebase Remote Config

Firebase Remote Config is a powerful tool that allows you to remotely configure and personalize your app without requiring users to update their app installations. With Remote Config, you can deliver tailored experiences to different user segments, perform A/B testing, and manage feature flags. This section will provide an overview of Remote Config and how to get started with it.

12.1: Introduction to Remote Configuration

Firebase Remote Config is designed to address several common challenges in mobile and web app development:

1. Personalization: You can tailor the user experience by adjusting the app's behavior, appearance, or content for different user segments. For example, you can change the app's theme for new users to make it more appealing.

2. A/B Testing: Remote Config enables you to run A/B tests without app updates. You can experiment with variations of app features or UI elements and measure their impact on user engagement and conversion rates.

3. Feature Flags: Managing feature flags allows you to control the availability of certain features in your app. This is especially useful for rolling out new features gradually or disabling problematic functionality.

4. Dynamic Content: You can update app content in real-time, such as promotional banners or in-app messages, without releasing a new app version.

5. Instant Updates: Remote Config changes take effect as soon as the app fetches the configuration from Firebase, typically during app startup. This means you can respond quickly to changing requirements or unforeseen issues.

To use Firebase Remote Config effectively, follow these steps:

Step 1: Set Up Firebase Project

If you haven't already, create or select a Firebase project in the Firebase Console. Remote Config is one of the Firebase services, and you need a Firebase project to use it.

Step 2: Install Firebase SDK

Add the Firebase SDK to your app by including the necessary dependencies and initializing Firebase. Make sure you follow the platform-specific setup instructions provided in the Firebase documentation.

Step 3: Define Parameters

In the Firebase Console, define the parameters you want to configure remotely. Parameters can be of different types, such as strings, numbers, or booleans, and you can set their default values.

Step 4: Fetch and Apply Configuration

In your app code, fetch the Remote Config parameters and apply them to your app's behavior or UI. You can control when and how often the app fetches the configuration to balance network usage and responsiveness.

Step 5: Monitor and Analyze

Use the Firebase Console to monitor how your Remote Config parameters are performing. Track user engagement, conversion rates, and other relevant metrics to evaluate the impact of your configuration changes.

Here's an example of fetching and applying a Remote Config parameter in an Android app:

```java
// Fetch Remote Config values
FirebaseRemoteConfig mFirebaseRemoteConfig = FirebaseRemoteConfig.getInstance();
mFirebaseRemoteConfig.fetchAndActivate()
    .addOnCompleteListener(this, task -> {
        if (task.isSuccessful()) {
            // Apply fetched values to your app
            int buttonColor = (int) mFirebaseRemoteConfig.getLong("button_color");

            updateButtonColor(buttonColor);
        } else {
            // Handle fetch error
        }
    });
```

In this example, we fetch the "button_color" parameter and update the button's color based on the fetched value.

Firebase Remote Config provides a versatile way to manage and customize your app's behavior and appearance without releasing app updates. Whether you're personalizing content, conducting A/B tests, or controlling feature flags, Remote Config can help you create a more dynamic and user-focused app experience.

12.2: Implementing Feature Flags and A/B Testing

Firebase Remote Config offers a powerful feature known as feature flags or feature toggles, which enables you to control the availability of specific features or functionalities within your app. This is particularly useful for gradual feature rollouts, enabling or disabling features for specific user segments, and conducting A/B tests to evaluate the impact of different feature variations.

Feature Flags

Feature flags, also known as feature toggles or switches, allow you to conditionally enable or disable features in your app without requiring a new app release. This is accomplished by defining a Boolean parameter in Firebase Remote Config that represents the state of a particular feature.

For example, you could create a feature flag named "new_feature_enabled" and set its default value to "false." Then, in your app's code, you can query this flag to determine whether to enable or disable the new feature:

```java
FirebaseRemoteConfig mFirebaseRemoteConfig = FirebaseRemoteConfig.getInstance();
```

```java
boolean isNewFeatureEnabled = mFirebaseRemoteConfig.getBoolean("new_feature_e
nabled");

if (isNewFeatureEnabled) {
    // Enable the new feature
    // ...
} else {
    // Disable the new feature
    // ...
}
```

By utilizing feature flags, you can easily toggle features on or off for different user segments or perform controlled feature rollouts. This allows you to manage risk, gather user feedback, and monitor the performance of new features in real-time.

A/B Testing

A/B testing, also known as split testing, is a common practice in app development where you experiment with different variations of a feature or user interface to determine which one performs better in terms of user engagement, conversion rates, or other key metrics.

Firebase Remote Config makes it straightforward to conduct A/B tests by allowing you to define multiple variations of a parameter and randomly assign users to each variation. For instance, you could create an A/B test for your app's home screen banner by defining two variations: "variant_A" and "variant_B."

Here's an example of how to set up an A/B test in Firebase Remote Config:

1. Define parameter variations in the Firebase Console:

    -   Parameter: "home_banner_text"
    -   Variations: "variant_A" and "variant_B"
2. In your app's code, fetch and apply the parameter, which will be randomly assigned to users:

```java
FirebaseRemoteConfig mFirebaseRemoteConfig = FirebaseRemoteConfig.getInstance
();
String homeBannerText = mFirebaseRemoteConfig.getString("home_banner_text");

// Display the home banner with the fetched text
showHomeBanner(homeBannerText);
```

3. Monitor and analyze user engagement with each variation in the Firebase Console.

By leveraging A/B testing with Firebase Remote Config, you can make data-driven decisions about which feature or user interface variation performs best, ultimately improving your app's user experience and performance.

Firebase Remote Config simplifies the implementation of feature flags and A/B testing, allowing you to optimize your app's features and user interface based on real-time data and user feedback. Whether you want to gradually introduce new features or experiment with different variations, Remote Config provides the flexibility to manage and analyze these changes effectively.

12.3: Personalizing App Experience

Firebase Remote Config offers a powerful capability to personalize the app experience for individual users or groups of users. Personalization is a key aspect of enhancing user engagement, retention, and satisfaction. In this section, we'll explore how you can leverage Firebase Remote Config to tailor your app's content, features, and messaging based on user attributes and behaviors.

User Segmentation

User segmentation is the process of categorizing your app's user base into distinct groups based on specific criteria or attributes. These criteria can include demographic information, user preferences, behaviors, location, and more. By segmenting your users effectively, you can target them with personalized content and experiences.

Firebase Remote Config allows you to define parameters for different user segments and set personalized values for each segment. For example, you could define a parameter called "welcome_message" and create variations for different user segments such as "new_users" and "returning_users."

```java
FirebaseRemoteConfig mFirebaseRemoteConfig = FirebaseRemoteConfig.getInstance
();

// Define welcome messages for different user segments
Map<String, Object> defaultWelcomeMessages = new HashMap<>();
defaultWelcomeMessages.put("new_users", "Welcome to our app! Get started with
our new user guide.");
defaultWelcomeMessages.put("returning_users", "Welcome back! Explore new feat
ures and updates.");

mFirebaseRemoteConfig.setDefaultsAsync(defaultWelcomeMessages);
```

By defining user-specific welcome messages, you can create a more personalized onboarding experience for new users while providing different messages to returning users to encourage engagement with new features.

Personalized Recommendations

Personalized content recommendations are a powerful way to enhance user engagement and drive user retention. Firebase Remote Config can be used to deliver personalized content, product recommendations, or news articles to individual users based on their preferences and past interactions.

To implement personalized recommendations, you can use Firebase Remote Config parameters to fetch content or product IDs that are relevant to the user. For example, you could have a parameter called "recommended_products" that contains a list of product IDs tailored to each user.

```java
FirebaseRemoteConfig mFirebaseRemoteConfig = FirebaseRemoteConfig.getInstance
();

// Fetch personalized product recommendations
String recommendedProducts = mFirebaseRemoteConfig.getString("recommended_pro
ducts");

// Display recommended products to the user
showRecommendedProducts(recommendedProducts);
```

By using this approach, you can create a personalized shopping experience or content discovery feature in your app, increasing the likelihood of user engagement and conversion.

Location-Based Personalization

Location-based personalization involves customizing the app experience based on the user's geographic location. Firebase Remote Config enables you to define parameters that vary by location, allowing you to display location-specific content or offers.

For example, you could have a parameter called "promotions" that contains location-specific promotions or discounts. By fetching the relevant promotion for the user's location, you can create a more contextually relevant user experience.

```java
FirebaseRemoteConfig mFirebaseRemoteConfig = FirebaseRemoteConfig.getInstance
();

// Fetch location-specific promotions
String locationPromotion = mFirebaseRemoteConfig.getString("promotions_" + us
erLocation);

// Display the promotion to the user
showLocationPromotion(locationPromotion);
```

Location-based personalization can be a valuable strategy for businesses that want to drive foot traffic to physical stores or offer region-specific incentives.

Firebase Remote Config empowers you to personalize the app experience by tailoring content, features, and messaging to individual users or specific user segments. Whether you're aiming to improve onboarding for new users, provide personalized recommendations, or offer location-based promotions, Remote Config's flexibility makes it a valuable tool for enhancing user engagement and satisfaction.

12.4: Managing App Configurations Across Environments

Managing app configurations effectively across different environments (e.g., development, staging, production) is crucial for ensuring a smooth development and deployment process. Firebase Remote Config offers features and best practices to help you streamline this process and maintain consistency in your app configurations.

Environment-Specific Configurations

In most app development scenarios, you have multiple environments, each serving a distinct purpose. The most common environments include:

1. **Development Environment**: This is where you and your team work on the app's features, fix bugs, and iterate on new functionality.

2. **Staging Environment**: Staging mimics the production environment closely and is used for testing before deploying changes to production. It helps ensure that everything works as expected in a controlled setting.

3. **Production Environment**: This is the live environment where your app is accessed by end-users. Changes should be thoroughly tested and validated in the staging environment before being deployed here.

To manage configurations across these environments, you can use Firebase Remote Config to create environment-specific parameter values. For example, you might have parameters like "api_endpoint" or "debug_mode" that have different values for each environment.

```java
FirebaseRemoteConfig mFirebaseRemoteConfig = FirebaseRemoteConfig.getInstance();

// Set different values for the same parameter in different environments
if (BuildConfig.DEBUG) {
    mFirebaseRemoteConfig.setDefaultsAsync(getDevelopmentDefaults());
} else if (isStagingEnvironment()) {
    mFirebaseRemoteConfig.setDefaultsAsync(getStagingDefaults());
} else {
    mFirebaseRemoteConfig.setDefaultsAsync(getProductionDefaults());
}
```

By setting environment-specific defaults for your parameters, you ensure that each environment accesses the appropriate configuration values.

Using Conditions

Firebase Remote Config allows you to apply conditions to parameters, allowing you to control which configurations are active in a given environment. Conditions are rules that specify when a parameter should be made available to clients.

For instance, you can create conditions like "debug_mode" or "is_staging_environment" and associate them with relevant parameters. When conditions are met, the corresponding parameters are made available to clients.

```
// Define conditions for parameters
mFirebaseRemoteConfig.setConfigSettingsAsync(new FirebaseRemoteConfigSettings
.Builder()
        .setMinimumFetchIntervalInSeconds(3600) // Set the fetch interval (e.
g., 1 hour)
        .build());

// Define conditions for parameters
mFirebaseRemoteConfig.setDefaultsAsync(getCommonDefaults());

// Apply conditions
if (BuildConfig.DEBUG) {
    mFirebaseRemoteConfig.setConfigSettingsAsync(new FirebaseRemoteConfigSett
ings.Builder()
            .setMinimumFetchIntervalInSeconds(0) // Force immediate fetch in
debug mode
            .build());

    mFirebaseRemoteConfig.activateFetched(); // Activate the fetched config i
mmediately
}
```

Using conditions allows you to have a central configuration that caters to different environments by activating the relevant parameters based on the environment-specific conditions you define.

Testing and Validation

Before deploying configuration changes to production, it's crucial to thoroughly test and validate them in the staging environment. Firebase Remote Config provides a testing mode that allows you to preview configurations without affecting production users.

During testing, you can use the Firebase console or the Remote Config REST API to fetch configurations for the staging environment and verify that they behave as expected in your app.

Versioning and Rollbacks

To maintain configuration integrity and facilitate rollbacks in case of issues, consider versioning your configurations in Firebase Remote Config. Each time you make significant changes, create a new version of the configuration.

In case of unexpected issues in production, you can easily roll back to a previous version to restore stability while investigating the problem.

Managing app configurations across different environments is essential for maintaining the quality and reliability of your app. Firebase Remote Config offers features like environment-specific configurations, conditions, testing modes, and versioning to help you achieve this. By following best practices in configuration management, you can ensure smooth transitions between development, staging, and production environments.

12.5: Best Practices for Using Remote Config

Firebase Remote Config is a powerful tool for managing app configurations, but to make the most of it, it's essential to follow best practices. Here are some recommendations for effectively using Remote Config in your Firebase project:

1. Plan Your Parameters

Before you start using Remote Config, plan your parameters carefully. Identify which aspects of your app should be configurable and which parameters need to be environment-specific. Having a clear plan will make your Remote Config setup more organized and maintainable.

2. Use Descriptive Parameter Names

Give your parameters meaningful and descriptive names. This makes it easier to understand their purpose and use, both for you and your team members. Avoid cryptic or ambiguous names that could lead to confusion.

```
// Good: descriptive name
mFirebaseRemoteConfig.getString("welcome_message");

// Bad: unclear name
mFirebaseRemoteConfig.getString("param1");
```

3. Employ Defaults

Always provide default values for your parameters. These values act as a fallback if Remote Config fails to fetch updated values. Having defaults ensures that your app remains functional even if there are issues with the configuration retrieval.

4. Test Thoroughly

Before deploying configuration changes to production, thoroughly test them in a staging environment. Verify that the configurations work as expected in your app and don't introduce any unexpected behavior.

5. Avoid Frequent Updates

While Remote Config allows you to update configurations without app updates, avoid making frequent changes. Frequent updates can lead to confusion and make it challenging to track configuration changes. Consider batching changes when possible.

6. Set Fetch Intervals

Configure fetch intervals wisely. Remote Config allows you to specify how often configurations should be fetched. For development environments, you might want to set a shorter interval for quick iterations, but for production, a longer interval is generally recommended to reduce unnecessary network requests.

```java
// Set fetch interval for production
mFirebaseRemoteConfig.setConfigSettingsAsync(new FirebaseRemoteConfigSettings
.Builder()
        .setMinimumFetchIntervalInSeconds(3600) // 1 hour
        .build());
```

7. Implement Versioning

Enable versioning for your configurations. This allows you to roll back to previous versions in case of unexpected issues or errors. Having a history of configurations is valuable for debugging.

8. Monitor and Analyze

Leverage Firebase Analytics to monitor how different configurations affect user behavior and app performance. Analyze the data to make informed decisions about configuration changes.

9. Documentation

Document your configurations and parameter meanings. This documentation can be valuable for you and your team members when managing configurations, especially in larger projects.

```java
/**
 * Configuration parameter: welcome_message
 * Description: The welcome message displayed to users on the home screen.
 * Default value: "Welcome to our app!"
 */
mFirebaseRemoteConfig.getString("welcome_message");
```

10. Secure Sensitive Data

Be cautious when using Remote Config for sensitive data. Avoid storing sensitive information, such as API keys or secret tokens, as configuration parameters. Instead, use a secure storage solution like Firebase Secrets or environment variables.

By following these best practices, you can effectively use Firebase Remote Config to manage your app's configurations, maintain stability, and provide a better user experience. Remote Config is a powerful tool when used thoughtfully, allowing you to adapt your app to changing requirements without the need for frequent app updates.

Chapter 13: Firebase Dynamic Links

13.1: Creating Deep Links for App Content

Firebase Dynamic Links is a powerful feature that allows you to create deep links for your app content. Deep links are URLs that take users directly to specific content within your app, even if the app is not installed. This is incredibly useful for user engagement, marketing campaigns, and improving the user experience.

What Are Deep Links?

Deep links are URLs that point to specific pages or content within a mobile app. They can be used to navigate users directly to a particular screen or view in your app. Unlike regular URLs, deep links can be opened either in a web browser or within the app itself, making them versatile and user-friendly.

Why Are Deep Links Important?

Deep links are essential for several reasons:

1. **Improved User Experience:** Deep links allow users to access the content they are interested in quickly, enhancing their overall experience with your app.

2. **User Engagement:** You can use deep links to guide users to specific features, promotions, or content within your app, increasing engagement and conversion rates.

3. **Marketing and Growth:** Deep links are valuable for marketing campaigns. You can share deep links on social media, emails, or other channels to drive user acquisition.

4. **Personalization:** Deep links can be customized to provide a personalized experience for users, showing them content that matches their interests or previous interactions.

Creating Deep Links with Firebase Dynamic Links

Firebase Dynamic Links simplifies the process of creating and managing deep links. Here's an overview of how to create deep links using Firebase:

1. **Set Up Firebase:** If you haven't already, set up Firebase in your project and configure it for your app.

2. **Create a Dynamic Link:** In the Firebase console, create a dynamic link. You can specify the deep link URL, the behavior when the app is not installed, and other parameters.

3. **Generate Short Links:** Firebase allows you to generate short links from your dynamic links. Short links are more user-friendly and easier to share.

4. **Handle Deep Linking in Your App:** In your app code, implement deep link handling. When a user clicks a deep link, your app should open the relevant content or screen.

5. **Track User Interactions:** Firebase Dynamic Links provides analytics to track user interactions with your deep links. You can measure the effectiveness of your links and make improvements accordingly.

Deep links can be used in various scenarios, including:

- **Onboarding:** Guide new users to complete their profiles or start using specific features after installation.
- **User Engagement:** Direct users to relevant articles, products, or services based on their interests.
- **Referral Programs:** Reward users for referring friends to your app with unique deep links.
- **E-commerce:** Share product links that take users directly to product pages, improving conversion rates.
- **Content Sharing:** Allow users to share specific content within your app with others.

In the next sections, we'll explore how to implement deep links, universal links, and track and analyze dynamic link performance using Firebase Dynamic Links.

13.2: Implementing Universal Links Across Platforms

Implementing universal links is an important aspect of utilizing Firebase Dynamic Links effectively. Universal links are a way to ensure that deep links work seamlessly across different platforms, such as iOS and Android, providing a consistent user experience. In this section, we'll explore how to implement universal links for Firebase Dynamic Links on both iOS and Android.

Implementing Universal Links on iOS

On iOS, universal links allow you to open specific content or screens within your app when users click on a link, even if the app is not installed. To implement universal links for Firebase Dynamic Links on iOS, follow these steps:

1. **Set Up Associated Domains:**

   - In your Xcode project, go to the "Signing & Capabilities" tab.
   - Enable the "Associated Domains" capability.

- Add your app's associated domains by specifying `applinks:yourdomain.com` in the format: `applinks:yourdomain.page.link` or `applinks:yourdomain.firebaseapp.com`.

2. **Configure Firebase Dynamic Links:**

   - In your Firebase project settings, make sure the iOS bundle identifier matches your Xcode project.
   - Download the `GoogleService-Info.plist` file and add it to your Xcode project.

3. **Handle Universal Links in AppDelegate:**

   - Implement the `application(_:continue:restorationHandler:)` method in your `AppDelegate` to handle incoming universal links.
   - Extract the deep link information and navigate the user to the appropriate content in your app.

Implementing Universal Links on Android

On Android, universal links are called "App Links," and they provide a similar functionality to iOS universal links. To implement universal links for Firebase Dynamic Links on Android, follow these steps:

1. **Configure Digital Asset Links:**

   - Create a Digital Asset Links JSON file that specifies your app's association with your domain.
   - Host this JSON file on your domain at `https://yourdomain.com/.well-known/assetlinks.json`.

2. **Configure Firebase Dynamic Links:**

   - In your Firebase project settings, make sure the Android package name matches your Android app's package name.
   - Download the `google-services.json` file and add it to your Android project.

3. **Handle App Links in AndroidManifest.xml:**

   - Add an `<intent-filter>` element with an `<action>` element for `android.intent.action.VIEW` in the appropriate `<activity>` in your `AndroidManifest.xml` file.
   - Specify the `android:autoVerify="true"` attribute to enable automatic verification of your app's association with the domain.

4. **Handle Deep Linking in Your App:**

   - Implement the deep link handling logic in your app to navigate users to the relevant content when they click on a universal link.

By implementing universal links on both iOS and Android, you ensure that users have a seamless experience when interacting with Firebase Dynamic Links, regardless of their device's platform. Users can click on a link and be directed to the appropriate content within your app, even if it's not installed, enhancing user engagement and retention.

13.3: Enhancing User Acquisition and Engagement

Firebase Dynamic Links offer powerful capabilities to enhance user acquisition and engagement for your mobile and web applications. In this section, we will explore strategies and best practices to maximize the benefits of Firebase Dynamic Links for acquiring new users and keeping existing users engaged.

1. User Onboarding with Deep Links

Leverage Firebase Dynamic Links to create a smooth onboarding experience for new users. When a user installs your app, you can use dynamic links to guide them through the onboarding process, ensuring they start with personalized content or features that are relevant to them.

Here's a snippet of how you can use dynamic links to navigate new users to specific onboarding screens:

```swift
// iOS (Swift)
if let dynamicLink = DynamicLinks.dynamicLinks().dynamicLink(fromCustomScheme
URL: URL(string: "yourapp://example?param=value")!) {
    if dynamicLink.matchType == .unique {
        let deepLink = dynamicLink.url?.absoluteString
        // Use the deep link to navigate to the appropriate onboarding screen

    }
}
```

2. Personalized Recommendations

Dynamic Links can carry user-specific information or preferences. Use this capability to offer personalized recommendations or content to your users. For example, you can generate a dynamic link that directs users to recommended products, articles, or videos based on their previous interactions.

```java
// Android (Java)
FirebaseDynamicLinks.getInstance()
    .getDynamicLink(getIntent())
    .addOnSuccessListener(this, pendingDynamicLinkData -> {
        if (pendingDynamicLinkData != null) {
            Uri deepLink = pendingDynamicLinkData.getLink();
            // Extract user preferences from the deep link and display releva
nt content.
        }
    });
```

3. Referral Programs

Implement referral programs to encourage users to invite their friends and colleagues to use your app. Firebase Dynamic Links make it easy to create referral links. Reward users who refer others with incentives, discounts, or exclusive content.

```javascript
// JavaScript (Web)
firebase.dynamicLinks().onLink(async (link) => {
    const deepLink = link.url;
    const referralCode = deepLink.searchParams.get('referral_code');
    if (referralCode) {
        // Award referral bonus to the referring user and the new user.
        // Track successful referrals for rewards.
    }
});
```

4. Cross-Platform Engagement

Firebase Dynamic Links are cross-platform, meaning they work seamlessly on both mobile and web. Leverage this capability to engage users across different platforms. For instance, you can send a dynamic link via email or SMS, and users can click it to open your app or website.

5. Campaign Tracking

Use Firebase Dynamic Links to track the effectiveness of your marketing campaigns. Create unique links for different campaigns, and analyze their performance using Firebase Analytics. This helps you understand which campaigns drive the most user engagement and conversions.

```javascript
// JavaScript (Web)
firebase.dynamicLinks().onLink((link) => {
    // Track campaign-related data and user interactions in Firebase Analytics.
});
```

6. A/B Testing

Experiment with different deep links and landing pages using Firebase Remote Config. A/B testing allows you to optimize your dynamic link content and layout for maximum user engagement. Firebase Remote Config lets you change the behavior of your dynamic links without publishing updates to your app.

Firebase Dynamic Links provide a versatile toolset for enhancing user acquisition and engagement. By tailoring your deep linking strategy to your app's specific goals, you can drive growth, improve user retention, and create a more personalized and engaging experience for your users.

13.4: Tracking and Analyzing Dynamic Links

Firebase Dynamic Links offer valuable insights into user behavior and the performance of your marketing campaigns. In this section, we will explore how to effectively track and analyze dynamic links to gain actionable data for optimizing your user acquisition and engagement strategies.

1. Firebase Analytics Integration

Firebase Dynamic Links seamlessly integrate with Firebase Analytics, allowing you to track user interactions with dynamic links comprehensively. To start tracking dynamic link events, ensure you have Firebase Analytics set up in your app or website.

```javascript
// JavaScript (Web)
firebase.analytics();
```

2. Standard Dynamic Link Events

Firebase Analytics automatically logs standard dynamic link events, such as when a dynamic link is clicked, opened, or the app is installed after clicking a link. These events provide essential data on link performance.

```javascript
// JavaScript (Web)
firebase.dynamicLinks().onLink((link) => {
    if (link.clickTimestamp) {
        firebase.analytics().logEvent('dynamic_link_clicked', {
            deep_link_url: link.url,
            campaign_name: link.campaign,
        });
    }
});
```

3. Custom Event Tracking

You can also implement custom event tracking for dynamic links to capture specific user interactions and behaviors. For instance, you can track when users complete a purchase or sign up after clicking a dynamic link.

```java
// Android (Java)
FirebaseDynamicLinks.getInstance()
    .getDynamicLink(getIntent())
    .addOnSuccessListener(this, pendingDynamicLinkData -> {
        if (pendingDynamicLinkData != null) {
            Uri deepLink = pendingDynamicLinkData.getLink();
            // Log custom events based on user interactions with the deep link.

            if (userCompletedPurchase(deepLink)) {
                Bundle params = new Bundle();
                params.putString("event_category", "ecommerce");
                params.putString("event_action", "purchase");
                firebaseAnalytics.logEvent("custom_purchase_event", params);
```

```
        }
      }
    });
```

4. UTM Parameters

Utilize UTM parameters to track the source, medium, and campaign of your dynamic links. Adding UTM parameters to your links allows you to identify which marketing channels and campaigns drive the most traffic and conversions.

```javascript
// JavaScript (Web)
const dynamicLink = `https://yourapp.page.link?utm_source=email&utm_medium=ne
wsletter&utm_campaign=summer_sale`;
```

5. Conversion Tracking

Firebase Analytics enables you to set up conversion tracking for dynamic links. This allows you to measure the success of your dynamic link campaigns by tracking specific user actions, such as making a purchase or achieving a certain engagement milestone.

6. A/B Testing Insights

If you are conducting A/B tests with dynamic links, Firebase Analytics can help you measure the impact of different deep links and landing pages on user behavior. Analyze the data to determine which variations are more effective in achieving your goals.

7. User Segmentation

Segment your user base based on their interactions with dynamic links. Firebase Analytics allows you to create user segments and analyze the behavior and characteristics of users who engage with your dynamic links.

8. Continuous Optimization

Regularly review your dynamic link analytics to identify trends, anomalies, and areas for improvement. Use the insights gained to optimize your dynamic link strategies, refine your targeting, and enhance your user acquisition and engagement efforts.

Tracking and analyzing dynamic links with Firebase Analytics is essential for making informed decisions about your marketing campaigns and user engagement strategies. By leveraging the data collected, you can refine your approach, improve conversion rates, and maximize the impact of your dynamic link campaigns.

13.5: Best Use Cases for Dynamic Links

Firebase Dynamic Links offer a wide range of use cases that can enhance user experiences, streamline marketing efforts, and improve app engagement. In this section, we'll explore

some of the best use cases for dynamic links to help you make the most of this powerful
Firebase feature.

1. Cross-Platform Promotion

Dynamic links are particularly valuable for cross-platform promotion. You can create a
single dynamic link that redirects users to the appropriate app store based on their device's
operating system. This simplifies your marketing efforts and ensures a seamless user
experience.

```javascript
// JavaScript (Web)
const dynamicLink = new firebase.dynamicLinks.DynamicLink('https://yourapp.pa
ge.link', 'yourAppName')
    .ios.setBundleId('com.yourapp.ios')
    .android.setPackageName('com.yourapp.android');
```

2. User Onboarding

Enhance user onboarding by guiding new users to specific pages or features within your
app. You can create dynamic links that deep link to onboarding tutorials, welcome
messages, or setup wizards, ensuring that users get the most out of your app from the start.

```java
// Android (Java)
FirebaseDynamicLinks.getInstance()
    .getDynamicLink(getIntent())
    .addOnSuccessListener(this, pendingDynamicLinkData -> {
        if (pendingDynamicLinkData != null) {
            Uri deepLink = pendingDynamicLinkData.getLink();
            // Redirect users to onboarding screens based on the deep link.
            if (isOnboardingDeepLink(deepLink)) {
                startActivity(new Intent(this, OnboardingActivity.class));
            }
        }
    });
```

3. Referral Programs

Implement referral programs to incentivize your users to refer friends and colleagues to
your app. Dynamic links can track referrals and provide rewards to users who successfully
bring in new sign-ups, expanding your user base.

4. Personalized Content

Deliver personalized content to your users based on their preferences or past interactions.
Dynamic links can be used to provide users with access to tailored content, promotions, or
recommendations, increasing engagement and user satisfaction.

```javascript
// JavaScript (Web)
const userPreferences = getUserPreferences(); // Retrieve user preferences
const dynamicLink = `https://yourapp.page.link?user=${userPreferences}`;
```

5. E-commerce and Discounts

For e-commerce apps, dynamic links can be used to share product listings, discounts, and shopping carts with customers. This simplifies the shopping process and encourages users to make purchases.

```javascript
// JavaScript (Web)
const productID = '12345'; // Replace with your product ID
const dynamicLink = `https://yourapp.page.link/product/${productID}`;
```

6. Event Promotion

Promote events, webinars, or conferences by creating dynamic links that provide users with event details, registration forms, and reminders. This is an effective way to boost event attendance and engagement.

7. Deep Linking

Dynamic links are an excellent choice for deep linking into your app. Whether it's opening a specific product page, a chat conversation, or a news article, dynamic links can take users directly to the relevant content, improving the user experience.

8. Abandoned Cart Recovery

For e-commerce apps, dynamic links can also be used for abandoned cart recovery. Send reminder emails or notifications with dynamic links that take users back to their abandoned carts, increasing the chances of completing the purchase.

9. User Feedback and Surveys

Gather user feedback and conduct surveys with dynamic links. You can create links that lead users to feedback forms or surveys, helping you collect valuable insights to improve your app.

Dynamic links are versatile and can be tailored to various scenarios and industries. By leveraging their capabilities creatively, you can enhance user engagement, boost conversions, and drive the success of your app or website. Experiment with different use cases to discover what works best for your specific goals and audience.

14: Firebase App Distribution

14.1: Distributing Pre-release Versions

Firebase App Distribution is a powerful tool that simplifies the process of distributing pre-release versions of your mobile apps to testers, stakeholders, and teams for testing and feedback. In this section, we'll explore the benefits and steps to distribute pre-release versions of your app using Firebase App Distribution.

Firebase App Distribution offers several advantages for distributing pre-release app versions:

1. **Effortless Distribution**: Easily share pre-release versions with internal teams, external testers, or stakeholders without the need for complex configurations.

2. **Cross-Platform Support**: Firebase App Distribution supports both iOS and Android, making it a versatile solution for teams working on multiple platforms.

3. **User Groups**: Organize testers into user groups, allowing you to target specific groups with different app versions and features.

4. **Instant Updates**: Quickly distribute new builds and updates to testers, ensuring that they always have access to the latest features and bug fixes.

5. **Feedback Integration**: Collect feedback directly within the Firebase Console, streamlining the communication between testers and developers.

To distribute pre-release versions of your app with Firebase App Distribution, follow these steps:

Step 1: Set Up Firebase in Your Project

If you haven't already, set up Firebase in your project. You can do this by creating a Firebase project and integrating the Firebase SDK into your app.

Step 2: Install Firebase CLI

Ensure that you have the Firebase CLI (Command Line Interface) installed on your development machine. You can install it using npm (Node Package Manager) with the following command:

```
npm install -g firebase-tools
```

Step 3: Authenticate with Firebase

Run the following command to log in to your Firebase account and authenticate the Firebase CLI:

```
firebase login
```

Follow the on-screen prompts to complete the authentication process.

Step 4: Initialize App Distribution

Navigate to your project directory in the terminal and initialize Firebase App Distribution for your app:

```
firebase init appdistribution
```

Step 5: Upload a Build

Build your app for testing and create a distribution package. You can do this for both iOS and Android apps. Ensure that you have the necessary build files ready.

Step 6: Distribute the Build

Use the Firebase CLI to distribute the build to testers or groups:

```
firebase appdistribution:distribute /path/to/your/app.apk --app your-app-id
```

Replace /path/to/your/app.apk with the path to your app's distribution package and your-app-id with your Firebase app's ID.

Step 7: Monitor Distribution

Monitor the distribution progress and collect feedback from testers through the Firebase Console.

Step 8: Update and Iterate

As you receive feedback and make improvements to your app, repeat the distribution process to provide updated builds to testers.

Firebase App Distribution simplifies the process of distributing pre-release app versions, allowing you to gather valuable feedback and ensure the quality of your app before its official release. Whether you're working on iOS, Android, or both, Firebase App Distribution offers a seamless solution for your testing and distribution needs.

14.2: Managing Beta Testing and Feedback

After distributing pre-release versions of your app using Firebase App Distribution, managing beta testing and collecting feedback becomes crucial for improving your app's quality. In this section, we'll explore the key aspects of managing beta testing and gathering feedback effectively.

Organizing Testers into Groups

Firebase App Distribution allows you to organize your testers into groups. Grouping testers helps you target specific sets of users with different versions of your app, configurations, or features. This feature is beneficial when you want to conduct controlled tests with specific user segments. To organize testers into groups, follow these steps:

1. **Create Groups**: In the Firebase Console, navigate to your project, and select "App Distribution." Under the "Testers" tab, click "Create a new group."

2. **Name Your Group**: Give your group a descriptive name that reflects its purpose, such as "iOS Testers" or "Feature X Beta Testers."

3. **Add Testers**: Select testers from your list of invited users or manually enter their email addresses. You can assign testers to multiple groups if needed.

4. **Define Permissions**: Specify whether the group members should have view-only or edit permissions for the distribution. Edit permissions allow testers to provide feedback directly in the Firebase Console.

Gathering feedback from testers is essential for identifying and addressing issues and improving your app. Firebase App Distribution makes it easy to collect feedback directly from testers within the Firebase Console. Here's how you can enable feedback collection:

1. **Enable Feedback**: In the Firebase Console, navigate to your project and select "App Distribution." Under the "Settings" tab, enable the "Feedback" option.

2. **Testers Provide Feedback**: Testers who receive your app build through Firebase App Distribution can provide feedback by clicking on the "Feedback" button in the app's distribution details.

3. **Review Feedback**: As feedback is submitted, it appears in the Firebase Console. You can review and respond to feedback to gather more details or clarify information.

4. **Track Feedback Status**: Firebase App Distribution helps you track the status of feedback, making it easier to manage and prioritize issues reported by testers.

As you receive feedback from testers, it's essential to iterate on your app by fixing reported issues, enhancing features, and making necessary improvements. Firebase App Distribution streamlines this iterative process:

1. **Develop and Test**: Use the feedback and insights from testers to guide your development efforts. Address reported issues and make updates to your app.

2. **Create New Builds**: Once you've made changes to your app, create new builds for testing. Ensure that you increment the version number to differentiate between builds.

3. **Distribute Updated Builds**: Use Firebase App Distribution to distribute the updated builds to testers, either to the same groups or new ones.

4. **Monitor Progress**: Continue monitoring feedback, tracking issues, and collecting insights as you iterate. Firebase App Distribution helps you maintain a streamlined feedback loop.

5. **Continuous Improvement**: The feedback loop with beta testers is an ongoing process. Regularly gather feedback, refine your app, and work towards a stable and high-quality release.

Firebase App Distribution simplifies the management of beta testing and feedback collection, enabling you to engage with testers effectively, address issues promptly, and ensure that your app meets the highest standards before its official release. By organizing testers into groups and streamlining the feedback process, you can iterate on your app with confidence and deliver an exceptional user experience.

14.3: Automating App Distribution Process

Automating the app distribution process is essential for saving time and ensuring a smooth release workflow. Firebase App Distribution provides various automation options and integrations that help streamline the distribution of pre-release versions to testers, making it easier to manage the testing phase efficiently.

Continuous Integration (CI) and Continuous Deployment (CD)

Integrating Firebase App Distribution with your CI/CD pipeline is a powerful way to automate app distribution. By doing so, you can automatically distribute new builds to testers whenever changes are pushed to your version control repository. Here's how to set up CI/CD integration with Firebase App Distribution:

1. **Choose a CI/CD Service**: Firebase App Distribution supports popular CI/CD services like Jenkins, CircleCI, Travis CI, and GitHub Actions. Select the one that best suits your development environment.

2. **Install Firebase CLI**: Ensure that the Firebase CLI is installed on your CI/CD server. You can use the Firebase CLI to authenticate and interact with Firebase services.

3. **Configure Environment Variables**: Set up environment variables in your CI/CD service to securely store Firebase credentials, such as the Firebase project ID and a service account key. These credentials are necessary to authenticate with Firebase.

4. **Automation Script**: Write a script or configuration file that automates the process of building your app, creating a distribution, and using the Firebase CLI to upload it to Firebase App Distribution.

5. **Trigger on Code Changes**: Configure your CI/CD pipeline to trigger whenever code changes are detected in your repository. This ensures that new builds are automatically created and distributed to testers whenever there are updates.

6. **Notify Testers**: Optionally, you can configure your CI/CD pipeline to notify testers automatically when a new build is distributed. This keeps your testers informed and engaged in the testing process.

Firebase App Distribution also offers a REST API that allows you to programmatically manage distributions. You can use this API to create and manage distributions, add testers, and upload new builds without manual intervention. API integration is beneficial for teams looking to incorporate Firebase App Distribution into custom workflows or tools.

To integrate with the Firebase App Distribution API, you'll need to:

1. **Obtain an API Key**: Generate an API key from the Firebase Console and configure the API key to restrict access to the Firebase App Distribution API.

2. **Make API Requests**: Use HTTP requests to interact with the API. You can create distributions, manage testers, and upload builds programmatically.

3. **Authenticate Requests**: Include your API key in the headers of your HTTP requests for authentication. This ensures that only authorized users can access the API.

4. **Handle Responses**: Parse the API responses to extract information about distributions, testers, and builds. You can use this data to keep track of your testing process.

By automating the app distribution process through CI/CD integration or API usage, you can significantly reduce manual tasks, improve efficiency, and ensure that testers have access to the latest builds promptly. This automation approach helps you maintain a well-organized and automated testing workflow, making it easier to iterate on your app and deliver high-quality releases.

14.4: Integrating with CI/CD Pipelines

Integrating Firebase App Distribution with Continuous Integration/Continuous Deployment (CI/CD) pipelines is crucial for automating the distribution of pre-release app versions to testers and stakeholders. It ensures that new builds are distributed seamlessly, enabling teams to receive timely feedback and streamline the development and testing process.

Here's how you can effectively integrate Firebase App Distribution with your CI/CD pipelines:

1. Choose Your CI/CD System

Select a CI/CD system that suits your project and development workflow. Popular choices include Jenkins, Travis CI, CircleCI, GitLab CI/CD, GitHub Actions, and Bitbucket Pipelines. Ensure that your chosen system supports the execution of custom scripts and CLI tools.

2. Install Firebase CLI

Make sure that the Firebase CLI is installed on your CI/CD server or runner. The Firebase CLI is a powerful tool for interacting with Firebase services, including Firebase App Distribution. You can install it using npm:

```
npm install -g firebase-tools
```

3. Configure Firebase Authentication

To securely authenticate with Firebase from your CI/CD environment, use Firebase service account credentials or a CI/CD-specific Firebase token. You can create a Firebase token using the Firebase CLI:

```
firebase login:ci
```

This command will provide you with a token that can be used for authentication in your CI/CD scripts.

4. Create CI/CD Scripts

Develop CI/CD scripts that automate the build, testing, and distribution processes. Your scripts should include the following steps:

a. Building the App

Use the build commands specific to your project (e.g., `npm run build` for Node.js projects or `gradlew assembleRelease` for Android projects) to compile your app.

b. Uploading to Firebase App Distribution

Use the Firebase CLI to upload the built app to Firebase App Distribution. Replace [YOUR_APP_ID] with your Firebase project's App ID, and [YOUR_TOKEN] with the Firebase token generated in step 3.

```
firebase appdistribution:distribute [YOUR_APP_ID] --token [YOUR_TOKEN] --release-notes "Release Notes"
```

c. Notifying Testers (Optional)

Optionally, you can use the Firebase CLI to notify testers about the new build:

```
firebase appdistribution:notify [DISTRIBUTION_ID] --token [YOUR_TOKEN]
```

5. Triggering CI/CD Jobs

Configure your CI/CD system to trigger these scripts automatically when changes are pushed to your version control repository. Typically, CI/CD systems provide hooks or triggers that respond to code commits and pull requests.

6. Monitor Distribution

Monitor the distribution process through Firebase App Distribution's web interface or programmatically using the Firebase CLI or API. You can track the progress of builds, view distribution metrics, and gather feedback from testers.

By integrating Firebase App Distribution into your CI/CD pipeline, you can automate the deployment process, ensure that testers receive the latest app versions, and accelerate the feedback loop, leading to faster development cycles and higher-quality releases. This integration is particularly valuable for mobile app development, where efficient testing and distribution are essential components of the development workflow.

14.5: Best Practices for App Distribution

Efficient app distribution is a critical aspect of the mobile app development lifecycle. It ensures that your app reaches the hands of testers, stakeholders, and eventually, end-users seamlessly and securely. Firebase App Distribution simplifies this process, but adhering to best practices can further enhance the experience and effectiveness of app distribution.

Here are some best practices to consider when using Firebase App Distribution:

1. Versioning and Release Notes

Always maintain a clear versioning strategy for your app. Use semantic versioning (e.g., 1.0.0) to indicate changes in your app's functionality and bug fixes. Alongside each distribution, provide comprehensive release notes. Clear release notes help testers understand what changes have been made and what aspects they should focus on during testing.

2. Distribution Groups

Leverage Firebase App Distribution's distribution groups feature. Create groups to categorize and manage your testers. For example, you might have separate groups for internal testers, external testers, and stakeholders. This allows you to target specific audiences for different types of releases.

3. Automation with CI/CD

As discussed earlier, integrate Firebase App Distribution into your CI/CD pipeline. Automate the distribution process so that new builds are distributed as soon as they pass automated tests. Automation reduces manual intervention and ensures that testers always have access to the latest version of the app.

4. Test on Real Devices

Whenever possible, test your app on real devices that represent the diversity of your user base. Firebase App Distribution supports distribution to both Android and iOS devices, enabling you to gather feedback on various platforms. Real device testing helps identify platform-specific issues that may not be apparent in emulators.

5. Collect Feedback

Encourage testers to provide feedback through Firebase App Distribution. The platform allows testers to submit feedback directly from the app. This feedback can be invaluable for identifying and addressing issues quickly. Ensure that you have a process in place to review and prioritize feedback.

6. App Permissions and Signing

Pay attention to app permissions and signing configurations. Ensure that your app's permissions are properly defined and that your app is signed correctly. These issues can lead to installation problems for testers.

7. Keep Distribution Links Secure

Distribution links generated by Firebase App Distribution are essentially public URLs that anyone with the link can access. While this makes distribution easy, be cautious about who has access to these links. Share them only with trusted testers and stakeholders to maintain security.

8. Monitor Distribution Metrics

Use Firebase Analytics to monitor how testers engage with your distributed builds. Track metrics like user engagement, crash reports, and user feedback. This data can help you make informed decisions about the quality of your app and prioritize bug fixes and feature enhancements.

9. Maintain Testing Environments

Create and maintain separate Firebase projects or environments for testing and production. This ensures that test data and configurations do not interfere with your production environment. Clear separation simplifies management and reduces the risk of accidental data leakage or misconfiguration.

10. Continuous Improvement

App distribution is not a one-time task but an ongoing process. Continuously seek ways to improve the efficiency and effectiveness of your distribution pipeline. Solicit feedback from your testing community to identify pain points and areas for enhancement.

By following these best practices, you can streamline your app distribution process, ensure that testers have a positive experience, and deliver high-quality apps to your users. Firebase App Distribution provides the tools and infrastructure to support these practices, making it an invaluable asset for mobile app development teams.

Chapter 15: Firebase AdMob and Monetization

15.1: Integrating AdMob for Monetization

Firebase offers various tools and services to help developers not only create great apps but also generate revenue from them. Firebase AdMob is one such service that allows you to easily monetize your mobile applications by displaying ads. In this section, we'll explore how to integrate AdMob into your Firebase project and use it for app monetization.

What is AdMob?

AdMob is a mobile advertising platform developed by Google that allows app developers to display ads within their applications. It offers a wide range of ad formats and helps you maximize your earnings by showing relevant and engaging ads to your users.

Benefits of Using AdMob:

1. **Revenue Generation:** AdMob provides a reliable source of income for app developers. You can earn money by displaying ads in your app.

2. **High-Quality Ads:** Google AdMob serves high-quality and engaging ads that match the interests of your users.

3. **Ad Formats:** AdMob supports various ad formats, including banner ads, interstitial ads, rewarded ads, and native ads, allowing you to choose the best fit for your app.

4. **Cross-Platform:** AdMob is not limited to a single platform. You can use it in both Android and iOS applications.

5. **Monetization Controls:** AdMob provides controls to customize ad settings, ad targeting, and ad delivery to optimize your revenue.

Integrating AdMob with Firebase:

To get started with AdMob, follow these steps:

1. **Create an AdMob Account:** If you don't already have one, sign up for an AdMob account on the AdMob website.

2. **Link AdMob to Firebase:** If you have a Firebase project, you can link it to AdMob in the Firebase Console. This integration allows you to access AdMob from the Firebase Console.

3. **Set Up Ad Units:** Create ad units in your AdMob account. Ad units represent the places in your app where ads will be displayed, such as banners, interstitials, or rewarded ads.

4. **Implement the AdMob SDK:** Add the AdMob SDK to your app's project. You can do this by adding the necessary dependencies to your app's build.gradle file.

5. **Initialize AdMob:** Initialize the AdMob SDK in your app's code. This is typically done in the onCreate method of your app's main activity.

6. **Load and Display Ads:** Use AdMob APIs to load and display ads in your app's user interface. You can choose the ad format that best fits your app's design and user experience.

7. **AdMob Policies:** Make sure to comply with AdMob policies to ensure your ads are displayed correctly and that you receive your earnings without issues.

Once you've integrated AdMob into your app, you can start earning revenue through ad impressions and user interactions with the ads. AdMob provides tools and reports to help you track your earnings and optimize your ad placements for maximum revenue.

In the following sections, we'll explore different ad formats, ad targeting, and strategies for maximizing your revenue with AdMob. Whether you're developing a free app or looking to generate additional income from your existing apps, AdMob can be a valuable addition to your Firebase-powered projects.

15.2: Ad Formats and Placement Strategies

In the world of mobile app monetization, choosing the right ad formats and placement strategies is crucial to maximize your revenue while providing a great user experience. Firebase AdMob offers various ad formats, each with its own strengths and use cases. In this section, we'll explore these ad formats and discuss effective placement strategies.

Common Ad Formats:

1. Banner Ads:

Banner ads are rectangular ads that are typically displayed at the top or bottom of the screen. They are non-intrusive and take up a small portion of the screen. Banner ads are best suited for apps with a lot of content, as they can be displayed without disrupting the user experience.

```
// Sample code to load a banner ad
AdView adView = new AdView(context);
adView.setAdSize(AdSize.BANNER);
adView.setAdUnitId("your_banner_ad_unit_id");
AdRequest adRequest = new AdRequest.Builder().build();
adView.loadAd(adRequest);
```

2. Interstitial Ads:

Interstitial ads are full-screen ads that are displayed at natural breaks in your app's content, such as between levels in a game or when transitioning between app screens. They offer higher engagement and can provide better revenue compared to banner ads.

```java
// Sample code to load an interstitial ad
InterstitialAd interstitialAd = new InterstitialAd(context);
interstitialAd.setAdUnitId("your_interstitial_ad_unit_id");
AdRequest adRequest = new AdRequest.Builder().build();
interstitialAd.loadAd(adRequest);
```

3. Rewarded Ads:

Rewarded ads are a user-centric ad format where users choose to watch an ad in exchange for in-app rewards, such as virtual currency, extra lives, or premium content. These ads can be highly effective at keeping users engaged with your app.

```java
// Sample code to load a rewarded ad
RewardedAd rewardedAd = new RewardedAd(context, "your_rewarded_ad_unit_id");
AdRequest adRequest = new AdRequest.Builder().build();
rewardedAd.loadAd(adRequest);
```

4. Native Ads:

Native ads blend seamlessly with your app's content and design, providing a non-disruptive user experience. They can be customized to match your app's look and feel, making them less intrusive and more engaging.

```java
// Sample code to load a native ad
UnifiedNativeAdView adView = findViewById(R.id.native_ad_view);
AdLoader adLoader = new AdLoader.Builder(context, "your_native_ad_unit_id")
    .forUnifiedNativeAd(unifiedNativeAd -> {
        // Populate the ad view with native ad content
        populateNativeAdView(unifiedNativeAd, adView);
    })
    .build();
adLoader.loadAd(new AdRequest.Builder().build());
```

Effective Placement Strategies:

1. **Consider the User Experience:** Always prioritize the user experience when placing ads. Avoid intrusive ad placements that can disrupt the flow of your app or annoy users.

2. **Use Interstitials Thoughtfully:** Interstitial ads should be placed at natural breaks in your app's content, such as when transitioning between levels or screens. Don't show them too frequently to prevent user frustration.

3. **Rewarded Ads for Value:** Implement rewarded ads in a way that offers real value to users. Reward them generously for watching ads to encourage engagement.

4. **Test and Optimize:** Experiment with different ad formats and placements to find the combination that works best for your app. Firebase provides analytics and A/B testing features to help you optimize your ad strategy.

5. **Ad Targeting:** Leverage Firebase Analytics and user insights to target ads to specific user segments. Showing relevant ads can increase user engagement and click-through rates.

6. **Ad Frequency Capping:** Limit the number of ads a user sees in a given time frame to prevent ad fatigue and maintain a positive user experience.

Remember that successful ad monetization involves finding the right balance between generating revenue and providing a pleasant user experience. Regularly analyze ad performance and gather user feedback to refine your ad strategy over time. Firebase AdMob provides the tools and flexibility you need to make data-driven decisions and maximize your earnings while keeping your users happy.

15.3: Maximizing Revenue with Targeted Ads

To effectively monetize your mobile app with Firebase AdMob, maximizing revenue is a top priority. One powerful strategy for achieving this goal is to implement targeted ads. Targeted ads ensure that the advertisements displayed to users are relevant and engaging, increasing the likelihood of clicks and conversions. In this section, we'll explore various techniques for maximizing revenue through targeted ads.

Leveraging User Data:

Firebase Analytics provides valuable insights into user behavior and preferences. By analyzing user data, you can create targeted ad campaigns that resonate with specific user segments. Here are some key strategies:

1. **User Segmentation:** Divide your user base into segments based on demographics, interests, and behavior. For example, create segments for users interested in gaming, shopping, or fitness. This allows you to deliver ads that align with each segment's preferences.

2. **Behavioral Targeting:** Analyze user interactions within your app to understand their preferences and behaviors. You can then deliver ads that match their interests and actions. For instance, if a user frequently browses fashion-related content, show them fashion-related ads.

3. **Geolocation Targeting:** Target users based on their geographical location. Promote local businesses or events by displaying ads relevant to the user's location.

The choice of ad format and placement also plays a significant role in maximizing revenue:

1. **Native Ads:** Native ads blend seamlessly with your app's content, providing a non-disruptive user experience. Customize native ads to match your app's design and layout, making them more engaging.

2. **Rewarded Ads:** Implement rewarded ads strategically, offering users valuable incentives for engaging with ads. The rewards can include in-app currency, power-ups, or premium content.

3. **A/B Testing:** Conduct A/B tests to evaluate the performance of different ad formats, placements, and targeting strategies. Use Firebase A/B testing capabilities to gather data and make data-driven decisions.

Ad mediation is a technique that allows you to optimize ad revenue by integrating multiple ad networks into your app. Firebase AdMob supports ad mediation, enabling you to maximize fill rates and eCPM (effective cost per mille). Here's how it works:

1. **Mediation Networks:** Integrate multiple ad networks, such as AdMob, Facebook Audience Network, and more, into your app through Firebase.

2. **Ad Requests Optimization:** When an ad request is made, the mediation platform evaluates which ad network is most likely to provide the highest revenue for that request.

3. **Real-Time Bidding:** Some ad networks use real-time bidding (RTB) to compete for ad impressions in real-time, further increasing revenue potential.

4. **Ad Network Waterfall:** The mediation platform can also use waterfalling, where ad requests are sent sequentially to different networks until an ad is filled.

5. **Unified Reporting:** Firebase provides unified reporting and analytics for all integrated ad networks, making it easier to track performance and revenue.

Regularly test different ad placements and strategies to optimize revenue without compromising the user experience. Here are some tips for effective ad placement testing:

1. **Frequency Capping:** Limit the number of ads a user sees within a specific time frame to prevent ad fatigue and annoyance.

2. **Ad Refresh Rates:** Experiment with ad refresh rates to find the ideal balance between showing ads and maintaining user engagement.

3. **User Feedback:** Collect user feedback to gauge their satisfaction with ad placements. Make adjustments based on their input.

4. **Performance Metrics:** Monitor key performance metrics, such as click-through rates (CTR), revenue per user (RPU), and eCPM, to assess the effectiveness of your ad strategies.

By combining user data analysis, strategic ad placement, ad mediation, and continuous testing, you can maximize revenue while delivering a positive user experience in your Firebase-powered mobile app. Targeted ads that resonate with users are more likely to result in higher engagement and increased revenue, making Firebase AdMob an essential tool for app developers and publishers.

15.4: Understanding AdMob Analytics

Firebase AdMob provides a comprehensive set of analytics tools to help you gain insights into your ad performance and user engagement. Understanding AdMob Analytics is crucial for optimizing your ad revenue and improving the user experience. In this section, we'll delve into the key aspects of AdMob Analytics and how to leverage them effectively.

AdMob Analytics Dashboard:

The AdMob Analytics dashboard offers a centralized view of your ad performance, providing valuable data and metrics. Here's an overview of what you can find on the dashboard:

1. **Total Revenue:** Monitor your total ad revenue, which includes earnings from various ad formats and networks.

2. **Ad Requests:** Track the number of ad requests made by users, helping you understand ad demand.

3. **Impressions:** Measure the number of ad impressions delivered to users.

4. **Clicks:** Keep an eye on the click-through rate (CTR) to gauge how engaging your ads are.

5. **eCPM:** Effective cost per mille (eCPM) represents your estimated earnings per thousand impressions, allowing you to compare performance across different networks and formats.

6. **Fill Rate:** Understand the percentage of ad requests that result in filled impressions.

AdMob Analytics offers customization options for creating reports tailored to your specific needs. You can define date ranges, filter data by ad units or ad sources, and segment the data by dimensions like country, platform, and ad format. Custom reporting allows you to dig deeper into your ad performance and identify trends.

User Engagement Metrics:

Beyond ad revenue, AdMob Analytics provides insights into user engagement, which is crucial for maximizing revenue. Key user engagement metrics include:

1. **User Sessions:** Track the number of sessions users have within your app, helping you understand how frequently they interact with your content.

2. **Screen Views:** Measure the number of times users view specific screens or pages within your app.

3. **Active Users:** Monitor the number of active users over time to assess user retention.

Mediation Analysis:

For apps that use ad mediation, AdMob Analytics provides detailed mediation reports. These reports offer insights into how different ad networks and sources contribute to your ad revenue. You can identify which networks perform best and make informed decisions about optimizing your mediation strategy.

Ad Unit Analysis:

AdMob Analytics allows you to analyze the performance of individual ad units within your app. By tracking metrics such as eCPM, fill rate, and CTR for each ad unit, you can identify high-performing units and areas for improvement.

Ad Format Testing:

To maximize ad revenue, consider experimenting with different ad formats, such as banner ads, interstitial ads, rewarded ads, and native ads. AdMob Analytics can help you evaluate the effectiveness of each format by providing data on ad impressions, clicks, and revenue generated by each format.

AdMob Integration with Firebase:

Firebase provides a unified platform for app development and analytics. By integrating AdMob with Firebase, you can correlate ad performance with user behavior, enabling more data-driven decisions. Firebase offers additional tools for user engagement, such as push notifications and A/B testing, which can complement your ad monetization strategy.

In conclusion, mastering AdMob Analytics is essential for app developers and publishers looking to maximize their ad revenue and provide a better user experience. By monitoring key metrics, customizing reports, and analyzing user engagement, you can fine-tune your ad strategy and make informed decisions that lead to higher revenue and user satisfaction.

15.5: Ethical Considerations in App Monetization

As developers and publishers, it's important to consider ethical principles when monetizing your mobile apps, particularly when using advertising as a revenue stream. While ads can be a legitimate and valuable source of income, they should be implemented in ways that prioritize user experience, privacy, and trust. In this section, we'll explore some key ethical considerations to keep in mind when implementing ad monetization strategies.

1. User Experience Matters:
- **Non-Intrusive Ads:** Ensure that ads do not disrupt the user experience. Avoid implementing ads that pop up suddenly, cover essential content, or hinder app functionality.

- **Frequency Control:** Limit the frequency of ads to prevent overwhelming users with excessive ad displays. Users should not feel bombarded by ads while using your app.

2. Respect User Privacy:
- **Data Collection Transparency:** Clearly inform users about the data you collect for ad targeting and personalization. Comply with data privacy regulations such as GDPR and CCPA.

- **Obtain Consent:** Obtain explicit user consent for data collection and ad personalization. Allow users to opt in or out of data-sharing practices.

3. Age-Appropriate Content:
- **Child-Safe Ads:** If your app targets children or has a significant child audience, ensure that ads displayed are appropriate for their age group. Advertisements should not contain explicit or harmful content.

4. Ad Transparency:
- **Label Ads Clearly:** Clearly distinguish ads from your app's content. Use labels like "Ad" or "Sponsored" to prevent confusion.

- **Avoid Deceptive Practices:** Do not use misleading or deceptive tactics in ad creatives or calls to action. Users should know what to expect when interacting with ads.

5. Ad Relevance and Quality:
- **Ensure Relevance:** Show ads that are relevant to your app's audience and content. Irrelevant ads can frustrate users and reduce engagement.

- **Monitor Ad Quality:** Regularly review the quality of ads displayed in your app. Report and block low-quality or inappropriate ads.

- **Implement Ad Fraud Measures:** Protect your app and users from ad fraud, such as click fraud and impression fraud. Use reputable ad networks and fraud detection tools.

- **Respect User Choices:** If users employ ad blockers, respect their choice and do not attempt to circumvent ad-blocking technologies.

- **Accessible Ad Formats:** Ensure that ad formats are accessible to users with disabilities. This includes providing alternative text for images and using readable fonts and colors.

- **User Feedback:** Encourage users to provide feedback on ads within your app. Act on legitimate concerns and continuously improve the ad experience.

- **Transparency in Revenue:** Provide transparency about how ad revenue is used to support your app's development and maintenance. Users appreciate knowing how their engagement contributes to your app's sustainability.

By adhering to these ethical considerations, you can create a positive ad experience for your users while maintaining trust and respect. Remember that a user-centered approach to ad monetization not only benefits your users but also fosters long-term success for your app by building a loyal and satisfied user base. Ethical app monetization practices contribute to a healthier ecosystem and help ensure the sustainability of your mobile app business.

Chapter 16: Firebase Extensions

Chapter 16: Firebase Extensions

Section 16.1: Overview of Available Extensions

Firebase Extensions are pre-packaged solutions that automate common development tasks and streamline your Firebase project workflow. These extensions can help you save time and effort by simplifying complex tasks, reducing the need for custom code, and ensuring best practices.

Firebase offers a growing collection of extensions that cover various use cases across different Firebase services. Here's an overview of some of the available extensions:

1. Image Optimization

The Image Optimization extension automatically resizes and optimizes images uploaded to Firebase Storage. It ensures that your images are served in the appropriate size and format, reducing load times and bandwidth costs for your users.

2. Firestore Full-Text Search

This extension enhances the search capabilities of Firestore by enabling full-text search on your Firestore documents. It uses Algolia, a powerful search engine, to provide fast and accurate search results.

3. Google Analytics Data Import

With this extension, you can import data from external sources into Google Analytics for Firebase. It allows you to combine data from various platforms and gain a holistic view of user behavior and app performance.

4. Realtime Database to Firestore

Migrating data from the Realtime Database to Firestore can be challenging, but this extension simplifies the process. It helps you transfer data seamlessly while preserving the structure and integrity of your data.

5. User Authentication Triggers

Managing user authentication events can be crucial for security and analytics. This extension triggers Cloud Functions in response to user sign-up and sign-in events, making it easier to automate tasks and maintain user records.

6. Slack Notifications

Stay informed about important events in your Firebase project by sending notifications to Slack channels. This extension allows you to set up custom alerts and notifications for various Firebase services.

7. Firebase to BigQuery

If you want to analyze your Firebase data with BigQuery, this extension simplifies the data export process. It automatically exports your Firebase data to BigQuery, making it available for advanced analytics and reporting.

8. SendGrid Email

Streamline your email communication by integrating SendGrid with Firebase. This extension enables you to send transactional and marketing emails to your users with ease.

9. Translate Text

For multilingual apps, this extension offers automatic translation of text stored in Firestore or the Realtime Database. It helps you provide content in multiple languages without manual translation efforts.

10. Cloudinary Image Upload

This extension allows you to upload images to Cloudinary directly from Firebase Storage. Cloudinary offers advanced image management capabilities, making it ideal for media-heavy applications.

These are just a few examples of the available Firebase Extensions. You can explore the Firebase Extensions registry to discover more extensions that cater to your specific project requirements. Extensions can be easily added to your Firebase project with a simple command, and you can configure them to suit your needs.

In the following sections of this chapter, we will delve deeper into installing, configuring, and customizing Firebase Extensions to enhance your project's functionality and productivity.

Section 16.2: Installing and Configuring Extensions

Firebase Extensions are designed to simplify your development process, and getting started with them is straightforward. In this section, we'll explore how to install and configure Firebase Extensions within your Firebase project.

Installing Firebase Extensions

To install a Firebase Extension, you need to use the Firebase CLI. Here are the general steps:

1. **Install Firebase CLI**: If you haven't already, install the Firebase CLI by running the following command in your terminal:

   ```
   npm install -g firebase-tools
   ```

2. **Initialize Firebase**: If your project isn't already initialized, navigate to your project directory and initialize Firebase by running:

```
firebase init
```

Follow the prompts to set up Firebase for your project.

3. **Install the Extension**: To install a specific extension, use the `firebase ext:install` command followed by the extension name. For example, to install the "Image Optimization" extension:

```
firebase ext:install firebase/storage-image-optimization
```

Replace `firebase/storage-image-optimization` with the name of the extension you want to install.

4. **Configure the Extension**: After installation, you'll be prompted to configure the extension. You can customize its behavior based on your project requirements.

Configuring Firebase Extensions

Configuration options for Firebase Extensions may vary depending on the extension's functionality. When configuring an extension, you can usually set parameters that define how the extension should behave. For example:

- **API Keys**: Some extensions may require API keys or credentials for third-party services. You'll need to provide these keys during the configuration process.

- **Storage Buckets**: Extensions like "Image Optimization" may require you to specify the Firebase Storage bucket where images are stored.

- **Trigger Events**: Extensions like "User Authentication Triggers" allow you to specify which authentication events should trigger Cloud Functions.

- **Integration Settings**: Extensions that integrate with other services may require you to configure integration details, such as setting up a SendGrid API key for the "SendGrid Email" extension.

Here's an example of configuring the "Image Optimization" extension:

```
? What should be the maximum image dimension (in pixels)? (press <Enter> to u
se the default) 1200
? What percentage of image quality should be maintained? (press <Enter> to us
e the default) 80
? What types of images do you want to optimize? (Press <space> to select, <a>
to toggle all, <i> to invert selection)PNG
? What types of images do you want to optimize? JPEG, PNG
```

In this example, the configuration prompts ask for the maximum image dimension, image quality, and the types of images to optimize.

You can view and modify the configurations of installed extensions in your `firebase.json` file. This file is typically located in the root directory of your Firebase project.

```json
{
  "hosting": {
    "public": "public",
    "ignore": [
      "firebase.json",
      "**/.*",
      "**/node_modules/**"
    ]
  },
  "extensions": {
    "image-optimization": {
      "maxDimension": "1200",
      "quality": "80",
      "supportedFormats": ["JPEG", "PNG"]
    },
    "another-extension": {
      // Configuration for another extension
    }
  }
}
```

You can manually edit this file to adjust extension configurations as needed.

That's the basic process of installing and configuring Firebase Extensions. Once configured, extensions can automate various tasks in your Firebase project, making development smoother and more efficient. In the following sections, we'll explore specific Firebase Extensions in more detail and demonstrate their usage in real-world scenarios.

Section 16.3: Customizing Extensions for Specific Needs

Firebase Extensions are incredibly versatile and can be customized to fit the specific requirements of your Firebase project. In this section, we'll explore how you can customize and extend Firebase Extensions to tailor them to your unique needs.

Extending Extension Functionality

Firebase Extensions come with predefined functionality, but you can extend their capabilities by modifying the code of the extension itself. This allows you to add custom features or adjust existing ones.

1. **Locate the Extension Source Code**: Firebase Extensions are open-source, and their source code is available on GitHub. You can find the source code for a specific extension by visiting the Firebase Extensions GitHub repository.

2. **Clone the Repository**: To make modifications, clone the GitHub repository of the extension to your local development environment.

   ```
   git clone https://github.com/firebase/extensions.git
   ```

3. **Customize the Code**: Once you have the source code locally, you can customize it to add new functionality or modify existing behavior. Be sure to follow any guidelines or documentation provided in the extension's repository.

4. **Deploy the Modified Extension**: After making changes, you can deploy the modified extension to your Firebase project using the Firebase CLI. Navigate to the extension's directory and deploy it.

   ```
   firebase ext:deploy
   ```

   This will upload the customized extension to your Firebase project, replacing the previous version.

Creating Custom Extensions

While modifying existing extensions is a powerful way to tailor Firebase Extensions to your needs, you can also create entirely new extensions from scratch.

1. **Set Up a New Firebase Extension**: To create a new extension, use the Firebase CLI to initialize a new extension project.

   ```
   firebase ext:init
   ```

   Follow the prompts to configure the extension and provide a name.

2. **Customize Extension Logic**: Once the extension project is initialized, you can customize its logic by editing the code in the project directory. You have complete control over the extension's functionality.

3. **Test the Extension**: It's essential to thoroughly test your custom extension to ensure it behaves as expected. You can use the Firebase Emulator Suite to locally test extension functionality.

   ```
   firebase emulators:start --only functions
   ```

4. **Deploy the Custom Extension**: When your custom extension is ready, use the Firebase CLI to deploy it to your Firebase project.

   ```
   firebase ext:deploy
   ```

   Your custom extension is now available for use in your Firebase project.

If you've created a custom extension that adds value to your Firebase project, consider sharing it with the Firebase community by open-sourcing it. This way, other developers can benefit from your work, and the Firebase ecosystem can continue to grow.

When sharing a custom extension, make sure to provide clear documentation and usage examples to help others understand how to use and customize it.

Customizing and extending Firebase Extensions empowers you to tailor Firebase to your project's unique requirements, making it a flexible and powerful platform for a wide range of applications. Whether you're modifying existing extensions or creating custom ones, Firebase Extensions can be a valuable asset in streamlining your development process.

Section 16.4: Automating Tasks with Firebase Extensions

Firebase Extensions can significantly streamline your development process by automating various tasks and workflows within your Firebase project. In this section, we will explore how you can leverage Firebase Extensions to automate common tasks and improve your project's efficiency.

Introduction to Automation with Firebase Extensions

Automation is the process of performing tasks, such as data processing, file handling, or notification delivery, without manual intervention. Firebase Extensions allow you to automate specific tasks by integrating pre-built or custom logic into your project. This can help reduce the time and effort required to perform repetitive actions, ensuring that your application operates efficiently.

Common Use Cases for Automation

Let's take a look at some common use cases where Firebase Extensions can be used for automation:

1. **Thumbnail Generation**: If your application involves user-uploaded images, you can use an extension to automatically generate thumbnails of those images, making them suitable for different screen sizes and devices.

2. **Data Backup**: Regularly backing up your database is essential to prevent data loss. Extensions can automate this process by creating scheduled backups and storing them securely.

3. **User Authentication**: Automate user authentication workflows, such as sending welcome emails or triggering actions based on user sign-up, with Firebase Authentication extensions.

4. **Notification Delivery**: Send notifications to users based on specific events, such as new messages or updates in your app. Firebase Cloud Messaging (FCM) extensions can handle this efficiently.

5. **File Cleanup**: If your application allows file uploads, you can set up an extension to automatically clean up expired or unused files from storage, helping to manage storage costs.

6. **Custom Triggers**: Create custom triggers that respond to specific events in your application. These triggers can execute custom logic to automate actions based on real-time data changes.

Deploying Firebase Extensions

To use Firebase Extensions for automation, follow these steps:

1. **Explore Available Extensions**: Visit the Firebase Extensions page to discover a wide range of pre-built extensions that can automate various tasks. Choose the one that suits your needs.

2. **Install the Extension**: Use the Firebase CLI to install the desired extension into your project. For example:

```
firebase ext:install <extension-name>
```

Replace `<extension-name>` with the name of the extension you want to install.

3. **Configure the Extension**: Configure the extension according to your project's requirements. You may need to provide environment variables or settings during the installation process.

4. **Deploy the Extension**: Deploy the extension to your Firebase project:

```
firebase ext:deploy
```

This will make the extension active and start automating the specified task.

Monitoring and Managing Extensions

Firebase provides tools for monitoring and managing your extensions:

- **Extension Logs**: View extension logs to monitor their activity and diagnose any issues.

- **Extension Dashboard**: Use the Firebase Console to manage extensions, including enabling, disabling, or removing them from your project.

- **Extension Updates**: Keep extensions up to date to ensure they benefit from the latest improvements and bug fixes.

By effectively leveraging Firebase Extensions, you can automate tasks, reduce manual effort, and improve the overall efficiency of your Firebase project. Whether you're working with user data, files, or notifications, there's likely an extension that can help automate and streamline your workflow.

Section 16.5: Community Contributions and Extension Development

Firebase Extensions offer a powerful way to automate tasks and enhance your Firebase project's functionality. However, there may be situations where you require custom automation or specific functionality that is not covered by pre-built extensions. In this section, we will explore how you can harness the power of the Firebase community and develop your own extensions to meet your unique requirements.

Community Contributions

One of the strengths of Firebase Extensions is the active and growing community that contributes to its ecosystem. Firebase users and developers often create and share their extensions, making them available to the broader community. These community-contributed extensions can be valuable resources to automate various tasks.

To explore community-contributed extensions, visit the Firebase Extensions GitHub repository or the Firebase Extensions Registry. Here, you can find extensions developed by other Firebase users, which you can use in your projects. When using community-contributed extensions, be sure to follow the installation and configuration instructions provided by the extension's author.

Developing Your Own Firebase Extensions

While pre-built and community-contributed extensions can be extremely useful, there might be scenarios where you need a custom solution to address your project's specific needs. Developing your own Firebase Extensions allows you to create tailored automation to meet your unique requirements.

Here's a high-level overview of the steps involved in developing your own Firebase Extension:

1. **Set Up Your Development Environment**: Ensure that you have the Firebase CLI and Node.js installed on your local machine. You'll also need a Firebase project to work with.

2. **Create a New Directory**: Create a new directory for your extension project and navigate to it in your terminal.

3. **Initialize Your Extension**: Use the Firebase CLI to initialize your extension project. You can specify the extension's name and other details during this step.

```
firebase ext:init
```

4. **Develop Your Extension**: Write the code for your extension. This code should include the logic required to automate the task or functionality you're targeting.

5. **Test Your Extension Locally**: Before deploying your extension, test it locally to ensure it works as expected. You can use the Firebase Emulator Suite to simulate Firebase services locally.

```
firebase emulators:start
```

6. **Deploy Your Extension**: Once you are satisfied with your extension's functionality, deploy it to your Firebase project:

```
firebase ext:deploy
```

7. **Configure Your Extension**: Configure your extension within your Firebase project, providing any necessary settings or environment variables.

8. **Monitor and Manage Your Extension**: Use the Firebase Console to monitor the activity of your extension and manage its lifecycle.

Extending Your Firebase Project

Developing custom Firebase Extensions enables you to extend the capabilities of your Firebase project beyond what is offered by pre-built extensions. Whether it's automating complex data processing, integrating with third-party services, or creating custom triggers, Firebase Extensions development empowers you to tailor Firebase to your project's exact needs.

As you embark on the journey of creating your own extensions, refer to the Firebase Extensions documentation and guidelines provided by Firebase to ensure that your extensions are well-documented, maintainable, and align with best practices.

In summary, Firebase Extensions provide a powerful means of automation for your Firebase project, and the community-driven aspect of extensions means you can access a wide range of functionality. When those options fall short, developing your own extensions allows you to craft bespoke solutions that precisely meet your project's requirements.

Chapter 17: Firebase for Enterprise Applications

Section 17.1: Scalability and Reliability in Enterprise Apps

In the world of enterprise applications, scalability and reliability are two fundamental pillars that can make or break a project's success. Firebase, with its suite of cloud services and infrastructure, offers robust solutions to address these critical needs. In this section, we will delve into the key considerations and strategies for building scalable and reliable enterprise applications using Firebase.

Understanding Enterprise Application Demands

Enterprise applications often cater to large user bases and require handling substantial data loads and traffic. Scalability, the ability to accommodate growing demands, is essential. Firebase's cloud infrastructure, which automatically scales to handle traffic spikes, provides a strong foundation for enterprise-scale apps.

Reliability is equally vital, as downtimes or data loss can result in significant financial and reputational damage for enterprises. Firebase services are built with redundancy and fault tolerance, minimizing the risk of service interruptions.

Firebase Realtime Database and Firestore for Scalability

Firebase offers two databases, Realtime Database and Firestore, both of which are designed for scalability:

- **Realtime Database**: This NoSQL database is suitable for real-time synchronization of data. It scales vertically, meaning you can increase database capacity by upgrading to higher-tier plans, which is suitable for many use cases. However, complex queries and high concurrency may pose challenges.

- **Firestore**: Firestore, a more recent addition, offers horizontal scalability. It automatically distributes data across multiple servers and scales horizontally with your application's needs. Firestore is well-suited for applications with extensive data requirements and complex queries.

Load Balancing and Traffic Management

Firebase offers load balancing features that distribute incoming traffic across multiple instances of your application. This ensures that no single instance becomes a bottleneck, providing both scalability and high availability. By default, Firebase Hosting uses global content delivery networks (CDNs) to serve content from the nearest edge server, reducing latency for users worldwide.

Autoscaling Cloud Functions

Firebase Cloud Functions allow you to run serverless code in response to events. With autoscaling, Cloud Functions automatically allocate resources to handle incoming events, ensuring that your application can handle spikes in usage. You only pay for the resources used during execution, making it cost-effective for enterprises.

Monitoring and Alerting

Firebase provides robust monitoring and alerting tools to help enterprises maintain the reliability of their applications. Firebase Performance Monitoring allows you to track app performance and set up alerts for critical issues. Firebase Crashlytics offers detailed crash reporting, aiding in quick issue resolution.

Security and Compliance

Enterprise applications often deal with sensitive data and must comply with industry-specific regulations. Firebase offers security features like Identity and Access Management (IAM), Firebase Authentication, and Firebase Security Rules to help you protect data and ensure compliance. Firebase is also certified for various compliance standards, such as SOC 2, HIPAA, and GDPR, making it suitable for enterprise use.

Advanced Enterprise Features

Firebase provides advanced features for enterprises, such as remote configuration with Firebase Remote Config, A/B testing, and personalization. These tools enable enterprises to adapt their applications to changing market conditions and user preferences swiftly.

In summary, Firebase offers a robust set of tools and services that are well-suited for enterprise applications. By leveraging Firebase's scalability, reliability, load balancing, monitoring, and security features, enterprises can build and operate mission-critical applications that meet the demands of modern businesses while ensuring data protection and compliance with industry regulations.

Section 17.2: Advanced Security Features

Security is paramount in enterprise applications, which often deal with sensitive data and must adhere to stringent compliance requirements. Firebase offers advanced security features to help enterprises protect their data and ensure the integrity of their applications.

Firebase Authentication

Firebase Authentication provides robust user authentication mechanisms, including email/password, social login, and multi-factor authentication (MFA). For enterprises, implementing secure user authentication is crucial to prevent unauthorized access to sensitive data and features.

MFA adds an extra layer of security by requiring users to verify their identity through a secondary method, such as a one-time password (OTP) sent to their mobile device.

Firebase supports MFA using SMS, email, or app-based verification codes, providing flexibility for enterprises to choose the most suitable option.

Firebase's Identity and Access Management (IAM) allows enterprises to control who has access to Firebase resources and what actions they can perform. IAM provides fine-grained access control through roles and permissions, enabling administrators to define access policies that align with their organization's security requirements.

By defining custom roles and assigning them to users or groups, enterprises can ensure that users have the appropriate level of access based on their responsibilities. IAM also integrates seamlessly with Firebase services, allowing administrators to manage access to Firestore, Realtime Database, Cloud Storage, and more.

Firebase Security Rules

Firebase Security Rules provide a declarative language for defining access control policies for Firebase resources. With Security Rules, enterprises can specify who can read, write, or modify data in their Firebase databases and storage.

Rules are defined using a simple and expressive syntax that allows for complex access control scenarios. For example, you can restrict access to certain data based on user roles, user IDs, or specific conditions. Firebase Security Rules are enforced on the server side, ensuring that unauthorized access attempts are blocked before they reach the data.

Data Encryption and Compliance

Firebase automatically encrypts data in transit using industry-standard TLS/SSL protocols, ensuring that data exchanged between client and server remains confidential. Additionally, Firebase provides options for encrypting data at rest, adding an extra layer of protection to stored data.

For enterprises that need to comply with specific regulatory standards, Firebase offers compliance certifications, including SOC 2, HIPAA, and GDPR. Firebase's commitment to data protection and compliance helps enterprises navigate the complex landscape of data security and privacy.

Audit Logging and Monitoring

Firebase offers audit logs that track user and administrator activity within the Firebase Console. These logs provide visibility into who accessed Firebase resources, made changes to security rules, or modified authentication settings. Audit logs are invaluable for compliance purposes and incident investigations.

Moreover, Firebase Performance Monitoring and Firebase Crashlytics offer insights into application performance and stability, helping enterprises identify and address security-related issues promptly.

Firebase Cloud Functions allow enterprises to run serverless code in response to events. To enhance security, enterprises can configure functions to run with specific IAM roles and permissions. This ensures that functions have access only to the necessary Firebase resources and data.

In summary, Firebase offers a comprehensive set of advanced security features that empower enterprises to build secure and compliant applications. By leveraging Firebase Authentication, IAM, Security Rules, data encryption, audit logging, and secure function execution, enterprises can protect their data, meet regulatory requirements, and maintain the highest standards of security in their applications.

Section 17.3: Managing Large User Bases

Enterprise applications often deal with large user bases, which can pose unique challenges in terms of scalability, user management, and performance. Firebase provides tools and features to help enterprises effectively manage and scale their applications to accommodate substantial numbers of users.

Firebase Authentication with Scalability in Mind

Firebase Authentication is designed to handle user authentication at scale. It can seamlessly authenticate millions of users while maintaining high performance and security. Firebase offers authentication methods such as email/password, social login, and multi-factor authentication to cater to various user preferences and security requirements.

For applications with a global user base, Firebase Authentication provides support for localization, allowing authentication flows to be presented in the user's preferred language or region. This ensures a user-friendly experience for diverse audiences.

User Management and Identity Verification

To manage large user bases efficiently, Firebase offers tools for user management. Firebase Console provides a user management interface where administrators can view and manage user accounts. This includes disabling, enabling, or deleting user accounts as needed.

Firebase also supports identity verification to maintain data integrity and user trust. Email verification and phone number verification are essential features for ensuring that users are who they claim to be. These verification methods can be integrated seamlessly into the authentication flow.

Firebase Realtime Database and Firestore

Firebase's Realtime Database and Firestore are NoSQL databases optimized for real-time data synchronization. They are well-suited for applications with large and growing user bases. These databases scale automatically to handle high concurrent read and write operations.

Firebase Realtime Database offers data synchronization in milliseconds, making it suitable for real-time chat applications, social networks, and collaborative tools. Firestore, on the other hand, offers powerful querying and indexing capabilities, making it ideal for applications that require complex data retrieval.

Firebase Cloud Functions for Scalable Backend Logic

Firebase Cloud Functions enable enterprises to offload complex backend logic to serverless functions. These functions can scale automatically to handle increased demand from a growing user base. Enterprises can use Firebase Cloud Functions to process user-generated content, trigger notifications, or perform other custom server-side tasks.

By integrating Firebase Cloud Functions with Firebase Authentication, enterprises can implement role-based access control and execute secure, scalable backend logic. This ensures that user interactions are processed efficiently and securely.

Performance Monitoring and Optimization

Firebase Performance Monitoring is a valuable tool for managing large user bases. It provides insights into application performance, including response times, latency, and network issues. Monitoring performance is crucial to identifying bottlenecks and optimizing the user experience.

By monitoring performance metrics, enterprises can proactively address performance issues, scale resources as needed, and ensure that their applications provide a responsive and reliable experience to users, even during periods of high traffic.

Load Testing and Capacity Planning

Load testing is an essential practice for ensuring that an application can handle the load of a large user base. Firebase Test Lab, combined with other load testing tools, allows enterprises to simulate heavy traffic conditions and identify performance bottlenecks and scalability issues.

Capacity planning involves estimating the resources required to support the expected growth of a user base. Firebase offers scalability features that can automatically allocate additional resources as traffic increases. Enterprises can fine-tune these settings to align with their capacity planning strategies.

In conclusion, managing large user bases in enterprise applications is a multifaceted task that involves user authentication, user management, scalable databases, serverless functions, performance monitoring, and capacity planning. Firebase provides a comprehensive suite of tools and features to help enterprises address these challenges and deliver a seamless experience to users, regardless of the size of their user base.

Section 17.4: Integration with Enterprise Systems

Enterprise applications often need to integrate with existing enterprise systems, such as Customer Relationship Management (CRM) software, Enterprise Resource Planning (ERP) systems, and Identity and Access Management (IAM) solutions. These integrations are crucial for streamlining business processes, enhancing data accuracy, and ensuring a unified user experience. Firebase provides several mechanisms for seamless integration with enterprise systems.

Firebase REST API

Firebase offers a RESTful API that allows enterprise applications to interact with Firebase services programmatically. This API is beneficial for integrating Firebase with existing enterprise systems that support RESTful communication. Using the REST API, enterprises can perform operations like creating, updating, or deleting data, managing user accounts, and triggering Firebase Cloud Functions.

To make authenticated requests to the Firebase REST API, enterprises can use Firebase Authentication tokens, ensuring that only authorized users and systems can access Firebase resources.

```javascript
// Example of making a REST API request with Firebase Authentication
const fetch = require('node-fetch');

const apiKey = 'YOUR_API_KEY';
const authToken = 'USER_AUTH_TOKEN'; // Firebase Authentication token

const headers = {
  'Content-Type': 'application/json',
  'Authorization': `Bearer ${authToken}`,
};

const data = {
  // Your request data here
};

fetch(`https://<YOUR_PROJECT_ID>.firebaseio.com/<YOUR_ENDPOINT>.json?auth=${apiKey}`, {
  method: 'POST', // or 'GET', 'PUT', 'DELETE', etc.
  headers: headers,
  body: JSON.stringify(data),
})
  .then(response => response.json())
  .then(data => console.log(data))
  .catch(error => console.error('Error:', error));
```

The Firebase Admin SDK is a powerful tool for integrating Firebase with enterprise systems that run server-side code. It provides programmatic access to Firebase services, enabling enterprises to manage Firebase resources, authenticate users, and interact with Firebase databases and storage.

By using the Admin SDK, enterprises can automate various tasks, such as creating user accounts, updating data, or monitoring Firebase services. Additionally, the Admin SDK supports various server-side programming languages, making it compatible with a wide range of enterprise systems.

```javascript
// Example of using the Firebase Admin SDK in Node.js
const admin = require('firebase-admin');

const serviceAccount = require('path/to/serviceAccountKey.json');

admin.initializeApp({
  credential: admin.credential.cert(serviceAccount),
  databaseURL: 'https://<YOUR_PROJECT_ID>.firebaseio.com',
});

// Access Firebase services using the Admin SDK
const db = admin.database();
const auth = admin.auth();

// Perform operations like creating a new user
auth.createUser({
  email: 'example@example.com',
  password: 'password123',
})
  .then(userRecord => {
    console.log('Successfully created new user:', userRecord.uid);
  })
  .catch(error => {
    console.error('Error creating new user:', error);
  });
```

Identity and Access Management (IAM) Integration

Firebase Authentication can be integrated with enterprise IAM solutions to ensure that access to Firebase resources aligns with enterprise identity policies. By enabling Single Sign-On (SSO) between Firebase Authentication and the enterprise IAM system, users can seamlessly authenticate and access both Firebase and other enterprise applications using a single set of credentials.

This integration enhances security, simplifies user management, and ensures that permissions and roles defined within the enterprise IAM system are respected within Firebase.

Enterprises often rely on CRM and ERP systems to manage customer data, sales, inventory, and other critical information. Firebase's Realtime Database and Firestore can be integrated with these systems through data synchronization and API calls.

For example, changes made in a CRM system can trigger Firebase Cloud Functions, updating corresponding data in Firebase. This bidirectional integration ensures that data remains consistent across systems, minimizing data entry errors and improving productivity.

In conclusion, Firebase offers a range of tools and methods for seamless integration with enterprise systems. Whether through REST APIs, the Firebase Admin SDK, IAM integration, or data synchronization, enterprises can leverage Firebase to streamline processes, enhance data accuracy, and provide a unified user experience across their applications and systems. This integration is essential for driving efficiency and competitiveness in the enterprise ecosystem.

Section 17.5: Case Studies: Enterprise Success with Firebase

In this section, we'll explore real-world case studies of enterprises that have successfully leveraged Firebase to achieve their business objectives. These case studies illustrate how Firebase's capabilities and features have enabled enterprises to address various challenges and drive growth.

Case Study 1: Streamlining Customer Engagement

Challenge: A multinational corporation operating in the retail sector faced a challenge in effectively engaging with its customers across multiple digital touchpoints. They needed a solution to unify customer interactions, track user behavior, and personalize the shopping experience.

Solution: The enterprise implemented Firebase Analytics to gain insights into customer behavior and preferences. They used Firebase Remote Config to personalize the app experience for different customer segments. By leveraging Firebase Cloud Messaging (FCM), they sent targeted notifications to users based on their browsing and purchase history.

Outcome: The corporation saw a significant increase in user engagement and conversion rates. By personalizing the shopping experience, they improved customer satisfaction and loyalty. Firebase Analytics helped them understand customer journeys better, leading to data-driven decisions and continuous optimization.

Challenge: A large manufacturing company with a dispersed workforce needed an efficient way to communicate and share information among employees. Traditional methods of communication were slow and lacked the necessary collaboration features.

Solution: The enterprise adopted Firebase Cloud Firestore to build a real-time messaging and collaboration platform for its employees. They developed a mobile app that allowed employees to send messages, share documents, and collaborate on projects in real time. Firebase Authentication ensured secure access to the platform.

Outcome: The company experienced a significant boost in employee productivity and collaboration. Critical information was accessible to employees in real time, reducing delays and improving decision-making. The platform streamlined communication across different departments and locations, enhancing overall efficiency.

Challenge: An e-commerce startup faced the challenge of building a scalable and reliable platform to handle rapid growth. They needed a solution that could manage product catalog updates, process orders efficiently, and deliver a seamless shopping experience.

Solution: The startup built their e-commerce platform using Firebase Cloud Firestore to manage product listings, Firebase Realtime Database to track order status in real time, and Firebase Storage to store product images. Firebase Functions were used to automate order processing and send order updates to customers.

Outcome: The startup successfully scaled their platform to handle high traffic loads during peak shopping seasons. Firebase's real-time capabilities ensured that customers received up-to-date information on product availability and order status. This resulted in increased customer satisfaction and repeat business.

Challenge: A financial institution with legacy systems needed to modernize its customer-facing applications while maintaining connectivity with existing backend systems. They faced the challenge of integrating Firebase with their legacy infrastructure securely.

Solution: The institution used the Firebase Admin SDK to create a bridge between their legacy systems and Firebase services. Firebase Authentication allowed customers to access their accounts securely. Firebase Cloud Functions were employed to trigger actions in the legacy systems based on user interactions in the new frontend applications.

Outcome: The institution successfully modernized its customer-facing applications, providing a more user-friendly experience. Firebase's flexibility and compatibility with various programming languages facilitated seamless integration with legacy systems. Customers benefited from improved online banking services while the institution retained its existing backend infrastructure.

These case studies demonstrate the versatility of Firebase in addressing diverse enterprise needs. Whether it's improving customer engagement, enhancing employee productivity, building scalable platforms, or integrating with legacy systems, Firebase offers a range of tools and services that can be tailored to meet specific enterprise objectives. These success stories underscore the value of Firebase in driving innovation and achieving business success in the enterprise sector.

Chapter 18: Cross-Platform Development with Firebase

Section 18.1: Firebase in the Multi-Platform Ecosystem

Firebase has emerged as a powerful and versatile toolset for developing applications across multiple platforms. In this section, we'll explore the importance of Firebase in the context of cross-platform development and its role in creating consistent and efficient experiences for users on various devices and platforms.

In today's digital landscape, users interact with applications on a multitude of devices, including smartphones, tablets, desktops, wearables, and even IoT (Internet of Things) devices. Developers face the challenge of creating and maintaining applications that work seamlessly across this diverse range of platforms. Firebase provides a unified backend infrastructure that simplifies cross-platform development, making it easier to deliver consistent features and experiences to users.

Here are some key aspects of Firebase's role in cross-platform development:

1. *__Shared Backend Services__: Firebase offers a common set of backend services that can be accessed from various platforms using platform-specific SDKs. This shared infrastructure includes features like authentication, real-time databases, cloud storage, and more. By using Firebase, developers can avoid duplicating backend code for different platforms, resulting in faster development and easier maintenance.*

2. *__Authentication and User Management__: Firebase Authentication provides a robust solution for handling user sign-in and identity management. Whether your application targets Android, iOS, web, or other platforms, Firebase Authentication allows users to sign in with their Google, Facebook, Apple, or email/password credentials, ensuring a consistent and secure authentication experience.*

3. *__Real-Time Data Synchronization__: Firebase's real-time databases, such as the Realtime Database and Cloud Firestore, enable synchronized data updates across all clients in real time. This is especially valuable for apps that need to maintain consistent data views across multiple platforms, ensuring that users see the same information regardless of the device they're using.*

4. *__Cloud-Based Storage__: Firebase Storage offers a scalable solution for storing and serving user-generated content, such as images, videos, and files. Developers can use Firebase Storage to manage media assets across all platforms, ensuring content consistency and efficient delivery to users.*

5. *__Cloud Functions for Serverless Logic__: Firebase Cloud Functions allow developers to write serverless functions that respond to events triggered by changes in the Firebase Realtime Database, Cloud Firestore, or other Firebase services. These functions can be triggered from any platform, enabling cross-platform automation and integration with third-party services.*

6. *__Cross-Platform Analytics__: Firebase Analytics provides insights into user behavior and engagement across all platforms. Developers can track user interactions, events, and conversions consistently, helping them make data-driven decisions to improve the user experience on each platform.*

7. *__Performance Monitoring and Optimization__: Firebase Performance Monitoring allows developers to monitor and optimize app performance across different devices and platforms. Identifying and addressing performance bottlenecks ensures a smooth user experience, regardless of the platform.*

8. *__Remote Config for Dynamic Adjustments__: Firebase Remote Config enables dynamic configuration adjustments without the need for app updates. Developers can tailor the app's behavior and appearance for different platforms, languages, or user segments, enhancing user satisfaction and engagement.*

In summary, Firebase plays a pivotal role in cross-platform development by offering a unified backend infrastructure and a comprehensive set of tools and services. Whether you're building applications for Android, iOS, web, or other platforms, Firebase empowers developers to create consistent and efficient user experiences while minimizing code duplication and maintenance efforts. This section will delve deeper into strategies and best practices for leveraging Firebase in cross-platform development, helping you unlock the full potential of this versatile platform.

It seems like you entered "FHUSSAIN," but I'm not sure what you would like to do with that input. Please provide more context or let me know how I can assist you further.

Section 18.2: Strategies for iOS and Android Development

When it comes to developing mobile applications, Firebase offers a robust set of tools and services that can greatly simplify the development process for both iOS and Android platforms. In this section, we'll explore some strategies and best practices for leveraging Firebase in your iOS and Android app development.

Firebase for iOS Development

1. Firebase SDK for iOS

Firebase provides a dedicated SDK for iOS, which includes all the necessary libraries and tools for integrating Firebase services into your iOS app. To get started, you'll need to add the Firebase SDK to your Xcode project using CocoaPods or manually adding the framework.

```
import Firebase
```

2. Authentication on iOS

Firebase Authentication simplifies user authentication on iOS. You can easily implement sign-up and login functionalities with email/password, social authentication (Google, Facebook, etc.), and more. Firebase Auth provides UI components for a smooth user experience.

```
Auth.auth().signIn(withEmail: email, password: password) { authResult, error in
    if let error = error {
        print("Authentication error: \(error.localizedDescription)")
    } else {
        print("User authenticated: \(authResult?.user.uid ?? "")")
    }
}
```

3. Realtime Database and Firestore

For real-time data storage and synchronization, Firebase offers the Realtime Database and Firestore. You can choose the one that suits your app's requirements. Both databases provide iOS SDKs for easy integration.

4. Firebase Cloud Messaging (FCM)

Firebase Cloud Messaging is Firebase's solution for push notifications. Implementing FCM in your iOS app allows you to send notifications to users, even when the app is in the background or closed.

5. Crash Reporting and Analytics

Firebase Crashlytics provides detailed crash reports for your iOS app, helping you identify and fix issues quickly. Firebase Analytics offers insights into user behavior, allowing you to make data-driven decisions.

Firebase for Android Development

1. Firebase SDK for Android

Just like iOS, Firebase offers an SDK for Android that simplifies integration. You can add Firebase to your Android project using Gradle.

```
implementation 'com.google.firebase:firebase-core:xx.xx.xx'
```

2. Authentication on Android

Firebase Authentication for Android is similar to iOS. You can implement various sign-in methods and customize the user interface for a seamless experience.

```
FirebaseAuth.getInstance().signInWithEmailAndPassword(email, password)
        .addOnCompleteListener(task -> {
            if (task.isSuccessful()) {
                FirebaseUser user = task.getResult().getUser();
                // User signed in successfully
            } else {
                // Authentication failed
            }
        });
```

3. Firebase Realtime Database and Firestore

For Android development, Firebase provides SDKs for the Realtime Database and Firestore as well. You can store and sync data with ease.

4. Firebase Cloud Messaging (FCM)

Integrate FCM into your Android app to send push notifications. Firebase Cloud Messaging is a powerful tool for engaging with users.

Firebase Crashlytics and Analytics are available for Android as well, helping you monitor app stability and user behavior.

In conclusion, Firebase offers comprehensive support for both iOS and Android app development. By following these strategies and using Firebase's SDKs and services, you can streamline your development process and deliver a high-quality mobile app to your users.

Strategies for Web Applications with Firebase

Firebase isn't limited to mobile app development; it's also an excellent choice for building web applications. In this section, we'll discuss strategies and best practices for using Firebase with web development.

Firebase for Web Development

1. Firebase SDK for Web

Firebase provides an SDK for web development, allowing you to integrate Firebase services into your web applications. You can include it in your HTML file like this:

```html
<script src="https://www.gstatic.com/firebasejs/9.4.0/firebase-app.js"></script>
<script src="https://www.gstatic.com/firebasejs/9.4.0/firebase-auth.js"></script>
<!-- Include other Firebase services as needed -->
```

2. Authentication on the Web

Firebase Authentication for web apps supports various sign-in methods, including email/password, social authentication, and single sign-on (SSO) with providers like Google and Facebook.

```javascript
const firebaseConfig = {
    apiKey: "YOUR_API_KEY",
    authDomain: "YOUR_PROJECT_ID.firebaseapp.com",
    projectId: "YOUR_PROJECT_ID",
    storageBucket: "YOUR_PROJECT_ID.appspot.com",
    messagingSenderId: "YOUR_MESSAGING_SENDER_ID",
    appId: "YOUR_APP_ID"
};


firebase.initializeApp(firebaseConfig);

// Sign in with Google
const googleSignIn = () => {
```

```javascript
const provider = new firebase.auth.GoogleAuthProvider();
firebase.auth().signInWithPopup(provider)
    .then((result) => {
        const user = result.user;
        // User signed in successfully
    })
    .catch((error) => {
        const errorMessage = error.message;
        // Handle sign-in error
    });
};
```


Firebase Firestore is an ideal database solution for web applications. You can use the Firestore JavaScript SDK to read and write data in real-time.

```javascript
const db = firebase.firestore();

// Add a new document with a generated ID
db.collection("users").add({
    name: "John Doe",
    email: "johndoe@example.com"
})
.then((docRef) => {
    console.log("Document written with ID: ", docRef.id);
})
.catch((error) => {
    console.error("Error adding document: ", error);
});
```


Firebase Hosting provides secure and fast web hosting with features like custom domains, SSL, and content delivery network (CDN) integration. You can easily deploy your web app to Firebase Hosting using the Firebase CLI.

Firebase offers real-time synchronization, making it effortless to update data and provide a dynamic user experience in web apps. Use Firestore or the Realtime Database for this purpose.

Just like in mobile app development, you can leverage Firebase Cloud Functions for web apps to add serverless functionality, integrate with third-party services, and automate tasks.

Best Practices for Web Development with Firebase

1. Security Rules

Implement Firebase security rules to control access to your data and ensure that only authorized users can read or write to your database.

2. Firebase Performance Monitoring

Monitor the performance of your web app using Firebase Performance Monitoring to identify and resolve performance issues, ensuring a smooth user experience.

3. Hosting Optimization

Optimize your web app's hosting by using Firebase Hosting's CDN integration and enabling caching for static assets to improve loading times.

4. Continuous Integration and Deployment (CI/CD)

Set up CI/CD pipelines to automate the deployment of your web app to Firebase Hosting whenever you make changes. This ensures a streamlined development workflow.

5. Testing

Don't forget to thoroughly test your web app on various browsers and devices to ensure cross-compatibility.

In summary, Firebase is a versatile platform that offers excellent support for web application development. By following these strategies and best practices, you can create secure, performant, and dynamic web apps that engage and delight your users.

Hybrid and Native App Development with Firebase

Firebase is a versatile platform that supports both hybrid and native app development. In this section, we'll explore the strategies and best practices for using Firebase in these contexts.

Hybrid App Development

1. Firebase and Ionic

If you're developing a hybrid app using the Ionic framework, Firebase can be seamlessly integrated. You can use the AngularFire library to work with Firebase services in an Ionic app. AngularFire provides AngularFireAuth for authentication and AngularFireDatabase or AngularFireFirestore for database access.

```typescript
import { AngularFireAuth } from '@angular/fire/auth';
import { AngularFirestore } from '@angular/fire/firestore';

constructor(
    private afAuth: AngularFireAuth,
    private firestore: AngularFirestore
) { }

// Authentication in an Ionic app
async signIn(email: string, password: string) {
    try {
        const userCredential = await this.afAuth.signInWithEmailAndPassword(email, password);
        const user = userCredential.user;
        // Handle successful login
    } catch (error) {
        // Handle login error
    }
}


// Firestore usage in an Ionic app
getItems() {
    return this.firestore.collection('items').valueChanges();
}
```

2. Firebase and React Native

For React Native, the `react-native-firebase` library allows you to integrate Firebase services. You can use this library to access Firebase Authentication, Firestore, Realtime Database, and more in your React Native app.

```javascript
import auth from '@react-native-firebase/auth';
import firestore from '@react-native-firebase/firestore';

// Authentication in a React Native app
async signIn(email, password) {
    try {
        await auth().signInWithEmailAndPassword(email, password);
        // Handle successful login
    } catch (error) {
        // Handle login error
    }
}


// Firestore usage in a React Native app
async getItems() {
    const snapshot = await firestore().collection('items').get();
    return snapshot.docs.map(doc => doc.data());
}
```

1. Firebase for Android

When developing native Android apps, Firebase offers a comprehensive set of Android SDKs for various services, including Firebase Authentication, Firestore, Realtime Database, Cloud Messaging, and more.

```java
// Firebase Authentication in Android
FirebaseAuth mAuth = FirebaseAuth.getInstance();
mAuth.signInWithEmailAndPassword(email, password)
    .addOnCompleteListener(this, task -> {
        if (task.isSuccessful()) {
            FirebaseUser user = mAuth.getCurrentUser();
            // Handle successful login
        } else {
            // Handle login error
        }
    });


// Firestore usage in Android
FirebaseFirestore db = FirebaseFirestore.getInstance();
db.collection("items")
    .get()
    .addOnCompleteListener(task -> {
        if (task.isSuccessful()) {
            for (QueryDocumentSnapshot document : task.getResult()) {
                // Handle document data
            }
        } else {
            // Handle query error
        }
    });
```

2. Firebase for iOS

For native iOS app development, Firebase provides iOS SDKs that offer similar functionality to their Android counterparts. You can integrate Firebase services like Firebase Authentication and Firestore into your Swift or Objective-C app.

```swift
// Firebase Authentication in iOS (Swift)
Auth.auth().signIn(withEmail: email, password: password) { (authResult, error
) in
    if let error = error {
        // Handle login error
    } else {
        // Handle successful login
    }
}
```

```swift
// Firestore usage in iOS (Swift)
let db = Firestore.firestore()
db.collection("items").getDocument { (document, error) in
    if let document = document, document.exists {
        // Handle document data
    } else {
        // Handle query error
    }
}
```

Best Practices

1. Offline Support

For hybrid and native apps, Firebase offers offline support. Ensure you configure your app to work seamlessly even when the user is offline, with automatic data synchronization when the connection is reestablished.

2. Firebase Cloud Messaging

Leverage Firebase Cloud Messaging (FCM) for push notifications in your hybrid or native apps. Keep users engaged and informed with timely notifications.

3. Cross-Platform Code Sharing

Consider code sharing strategies like React Native's "Write Once, Run Anywhere" approach or using libraries that allow code sharing between Android and iOS to reduce development effort and maintenance.

4. Testing and Debugging

Perform thorough testing on both Android and iOS devices, as well as emulators or simulators, to ensure your hybrid or native app functions correctly.

In summary, Firebase provides excellent support for both hybrid and native app development. By following these strategies and best practices, you can create high-quality apps that offer a consistent and engaging user experience across different platforms.

Future Trends in Firebase Development

Firebase is an ever-evolving platform that keeps up with the latest trends in app development. In this section, we'll explore some of the future trends in Firebase development and how they can benefit your projects.

1. Integration with Machine Learning and AI

As machine learning and artificial intelligence become increasingly important in app development, Firebase is expected to offer more integration with ML/AI services. Firebase's machine learning kit already provides features like ML Kit Vision, Natural Language Processing, and Custom ML models. In the future, we can anticipate even more advanced AI capabilities, making it easier to incorporate machine learning into your apps.

2. Enhanced Real-time Capabilities

Real-time data synchronization has been a core feature of Firebase, and it's expected to become even more robust. With the growing demand for real-time updates in applications, Firebase is likely to introduce improvements and optimizations to provide even faster and more reliable real-time data synchronization.

3. Serverless Computing

Firebase Functions, the serverless compute service of Firebase, is likely to see advancements. Expect improvements in terms of scalability, flexibility, and integration capabilities. Firebase Functions will continue to enable developers to build serverless applications without the need to manage infrastructure.

4. Better Analytics and Insights

Firebase Analytics is already a powerful tool for tracking user behavior, but it's expected to become even more sophisticated. Enhanced analytics features, including more detailed user insights and predictive analytics, will help app developers make data-driven decisions to improve their apps.

5. Cross-Platform Development

Firebase is positioned well for the growing trend of cross-platform development. With the rise of frameworks like Flutter and React Native, Firebase's support for these platforms is expected to improve, making it easier for developers to build high-quality apps that work seamlessly across different devices and operating systems.

6. Enhanced Security

Security is a top concern for app developers, and Firebase is likely to continue enhancing its security features. Expect more robust authentication options, improved data security, and advanced threat detection capabilities to protect user data and app infrastructure.

7. Edge Computing and IoT

As edge computing and the Internet of Things (IoT) gain momentum, Firebase may expand its capabilities to better support these technologies. Developers may be able to use Firebase to build and manage IoT applications more effectively, including handling real-time data from edge devices.

Firebase's testing and monitoring tools are expected to evolve, allowing developers to identify and fix issues more easily. Advanced testing automation, performance monitoring, and error tracking features will help maintain high-quality apps in the face of growing complexity.

In conclusion, Firebase continues to be at the forefront of mobile and web app development. By staying up-to-date with these future trends in Firebase development, you can take advantage of the latest features and capabilities to build innovative and high-performing applications. Keep an eye on Firebase updates and announcements to stay informed about the evolving ecosystem.

Custom Backend Services with Firebase

Firebase offers a wide range of backend services, but there are situations where you may need to create custom backend functionality to meet your app's specific requirements. In this section, we'll explore how you can leverage Firebase to build custom backend services that integrate seamlessly with your Firebase-powered application.

Firebase's backend-as-a-service (BaaS) capabilities, combined with Cloud Functions, allow you to create powerful custom backend services. Here are some scenarios where custom backend services can be beneficial:

1. Custom API Endpoints

Sometimes, your app needs custom API endpoints to perform tasks that Firebase doesn't directly support out of the box. You can use Firebase Cloud Functions to create serverless API endpoints that interact with your Firebase Realtime Database, Firestore, or other Firebase services.

For example, you might create an endpoint to generate custom reports, send push notifications, or perform complex calculations on your data. Here's an example of how you can define a Cloud Function that exposes a custom API endpoint:

```
const functions = require('firebase-functions');
const express = require('express');
const app = express();

app.get('/customEndpoint', (req, res) => {
  // Your custom logic here
  res.status(200).send('Custom endpoint response');
});

exports.customApi = functions.https.onRequest(app);
```

2. Integrating with External Services

Firebase allows you to integrate with external services and APIs to extend your app's functionality. You can use Firebase Cloud Functions to make HTTP requests to third-party APIs, process the data, and return results to your app.

For instance, you might integrate your app with a payment gateway, weather service, or social media platform. Firebase's serverless architecture makes it easy to manage these integrations without the need for a dedicated backend server.

3. Real-time Data Processing

Firebase provides real-time data synchronization, but there may be cases where you need to process data in real-time before storing it or sending it to clients. Firebase Cloud Functions can be triggered by database events and allow you to process data and trigger further actions based on real-time changes.

For example, you can create a function that triggers when a new order is placed in your app, processes the order data, sends notifications to users and admin, and updates the order status in the database.

4. Scheduled Tasks

Firebase Cloud Functions also enable you to schedule tasks that run at specific intervals. This is useful for automating repetitive tasks, such as sending daily email digests, performing database maintenance, or aggregating data for reporting.

Here's an example of scheduling a function to run daily:

```javascript
const functions = require('firebase-functions');
const admin = require('firebase-admin');
admin.initializeApp();

exports.scheduledTask = functions.pubsub.schedule('every 24 hours').timeZone(
'UTC').onRun((context) => {
  // Your scheduled task logic here
  console.log('Scheduled task executed.');
  return null;
});
```

5. Custom Authentication

While Firebase offers various authentication providers, you may have unique authentication requirements. Firebase allows you to implement custom authentication methods, integrating with your existing user management system or external identity providers.

Custom authentication can be achieved using Firebase Authentication triggers in Cloud Functions. You can create and verify custom tokens for your users, granting them access to Firebase services securely.

In summary, Firebase's flexibility and extensibility make it a powerful platform for building custom backend services that complement its core features. Whether you need custom API endpoints, external service integration, real-time data processing, scheduled tasks, or custom authentication, Firebase, coupled with Cloud Functions, provides the tools to create a tailored backend solution for your app.

Integrating Firebase with Machine Learning and AI

Integrating Firebase with machine learning (ML) and artificial intelligence (AI) services can greatly enhance the capabilities of your applications. Firebase provides the infrastructure to collect and manage data, while ML and AI can analyze and derive insights from that data. In this section, we'll explore how you can seamlessly integrate Firebase with ML and AI services to create intelligent and data-driven applications.

Firebase and Google Cloud Platform (GCP)

Firebase is built on top of Google Cloud Platform (GCP), which offers a wide range of ML and AI services. By integrating Firebase with GCP, you can leverage these services to add advanced features to your app. Some GCP services that work well with Firebase include:

1. *Cloud Machine Learning Engine: This service allows you to train and deploy machine learning models. You can use Firebase to collect and preprocess data, then train models in GCP, and finally deploy these models to Firebase or your app.*

2. *Cloud Vision API: It provides powerful image analysis capabilities, including label detection, face recognition, and optical character recognition (OCR). You can use Firebase Storage to store images and Cloud Vision API to analyze them.*

3. *Natural Language API: This service can analyze text for sentiment analysis, entity recognition, and language detection. Firebase can collect user-generated text data, and GCP's Natural Language API can extract valuable insights from it.*

4. *BigQuery: Firebase integrates seamlessly with BigQuery, Google's data warehouse. You can use BigQuery to run SQL-like queries on your data collected by Firebase, gaining deeper insights and performing advanced analytics.*

Collecting and Preprocessing Data

To make the most of ML and AI services, you need to collect and preprocess data effectively. Firebase provides real-time database solutions (Realtime Database and Firestore) that can store structured data, while Firebase Analytics can track user behavior and generate valuable insights.

Consider an e-commerce app. Firebase can collect data on user interactions, such as product views, purchases, and reviews. This data can be stored in Firebase and exported to

GCP for further analysis. You can also use Firebase Cloud Functions to trigger data preprocessing tasks and send clean data to GCP services.

Once you have collected and preprocessed your data, it's time to build and train ML models. GCP offers tools like TensorFlow and AutoML to create custom models. You can use Firebase Cloud Functions to automate model training whenever new data arrives.

For example, in a recommendation system, you can use Firebase to track user preferences and interactions with products. When a user's profile changes significantly, Firebase Cloud Functions can trigger model retraining in GCP. The updated model can then be deployed and used within your Firebase-powered app to provide personalized recommendations.

Firebase enables real-time data synchronization between your app and backend. This is invaluable when incorporating AI-driven features. For instance, you can use Cloud Functions to process user-generated content in real time.

Consider a social media app that analyzes user posts for inappropriate content. Firebase Realtime Database can store user posts, and a Cloud Function can be triggered upon new post creation. This function can use AI services like Cloud Natural Language to analyze the content and take actions such as flagging or removing inappropriate posts.

Integrating Firebase with ML and AI services is an ongoing process. It's important to monitor the performance of your AI models and gather user feedback to make continuous improvements. Firebase Performance Monitoring can help identify bottlenecks and issues in your app, while Firebase Remote Config can be used to fine-tune AI-related features without app updates.

In conclusion, Firebase's integration with GCP's ML and AI services empowers you to create intelligent and data-driven applications. By collecting and preprocessing data, training and deploying models, and delivering real-time insights, you can provide users with personalized experiences and valuable insights. Monitoring and iterating on AI features ensure that your app continues to evolve and meet user expectations.

Complex Queries and Data Aggregation

Firebase offers robust real-time database solutions that allow you to store and retrieve data efficiently. In this section, we'll explore complex queries and data aggregation techniques using Firebase Realtime Database and Firestore.

Firebase Realtime Database is a NoSQL database that allows you to store JSON-like structured data. When your data structure becomes complex and you need to query or aggregate data, Firebase provides tools and techniques to accomplish these tasks.

Querying Data

Firebase Realtime Database supports various query operations to filter and retrieve data efficiently. Some common query operations include:

- **orderByChild**: Sorts the data by the specified child key's values.
- **equalTo**: Filters data where a specified child key has a specific value.
- **startAt** and **endAt**: Retrieve data with values greater than or equal to a specified value or less than or equal to a specified value.
- **limitToFirst** and **limitToLast**: Limits the number of results to the first or last N records.

Here's an example of querying data in Firebase Realtime Database:

```javascript
// Query for all posts where the author is "Alice"
const query = firebase.database().ref('posts').orderByChild('author').equalTo
('Alice');

query.on('value', (snapshot) => {
  // Handle the results here
  const posts = snapshot.val();
  console.log(posts);
});
```

Data Aggregation

Firebase Realtime Database doesn't natively support server-side data aggregation like traditional SQL databases. However, you can perform client-side aggregation to compute summaries and statistics.

For instance, if you have a database of orders, you can retrieve all the orders and calculate the total revenue on the client side:

```javascript
const ordersRef = firebase.database().ref('orders');

ordersRef.once('value', (snapshot) => {
  const orders = snapshot.val();
  let totalRevenue = 0;

  for (const orderId in orders) {
    totalRevenue += orders[orderId].totalAmount;
  }
```

```js
  console.log('Total Revenue:', totalRevenue);
});
```

While this client-side approach works well for small to moderate-sized datasets, it may not be efficient for large datasets due to the limitations of client devices.

Firebase Firestore

Firebase Firestore is a more advanced NoSQL database that offers enhanced querying and data aggregation capabilities compared to the Realtime Database. Firestore supports complex queries and aggregation at the server-side, making it suitable for large-scale applications.

Querying Data

Firestore allows you to build complex queries using chaining methods. You can filter and sort data based on multiple criteria, making it versatile for various use cases.

Here's an example of querying data in Firestore:

```js
// Query for all cities in California with a population greater than 1 millio
n
const query = firebase.firestore().collection('cities')
  .where('state', '==', 'CA')
  .where('population', '>', 1000000);

query.get().then((snapshot) => {
  snapshot.forEach((doc) => {
    // Handle each document here
    console.log(doc.id, '=>', doc.data());
  });
});
```

Data Aggregation

Firestore supports server-side data aggregation using aggregation pipelines. You can perform operations like counting documents, calculating sums, and grouping data based on specific criteria.

Here's an example of calculating the total population of all cities in California using Firestore:

```js
const citiesRef = firebase.firestore().collection('cities');

citiesRef.where('state', '==', 'CA').get().then((snapshot) => {
  let totalPopulation = 0;

  snapshot.forEach((doc) => {
    totalPopulation += doc.data().population;
  });
```

```javascript
  console.log('Total Population in California:', totalPopulation);
});
```

Firestore's server-side data aggregation capabilities are beneficial for applications that require complex data processing and analytics.

In conclusion, Firebase Realtime Database and Firestore provide the tools necessary for querying and aggregating data efficiently. Firebase Realtime Database is suitable for simpler data structures and client-side aggregation, while Firestore excels in handling complex queries and server-side data aggregation for larger datasets. Choosing the right database for your application depends on your specific requirements and scalability needs.

Geo-distribution and Multi-region Setup

Geo-distribution is a crucial consideration for applications that aim to provide low-latency access to users across the globe. Firebase offers features and strategies to optimize geo-distribution and ensure that your application delivers excellent performance worldwide.

Firebase Realtime Database

In Firebase Realtime Database, your data is hosted on servers in a single location or region. While Firebase handles server management and scaling automatically, the database's geographic location can impact latency for users in distant regions.

To optimize geo-distribution with Firebase Realtime Database, you can consider the following strategies:

1. Choose the Right Region

Firebase allows you to choose the geographic location for your Realtime Database when creating a new project. Select a region that aligns with your target user base to minimize latency.

```javascript
const firebaseConfig = {
  apiKey: 'YOUR_API_KEY',
  authDomain: 'your-project.firebaseapp.com',
  databaseURL: 'https://your-project.firebaseio.com',
  projectId: 'your-project',
  storageBucket: 'your-project.appspot.com',
  messagingSenderId: 'YOUR_MESSAGING_SENDER_ID',
  appId: 'YOUR_APP_ID',
  measurementId: 'YOUR_MEASUREMENT_ID',
};

firebase.initializeApp(firebaseConfig);
```

You can further reduce latency by using Content Delivery Networks (CDNs) in combination with Firebase Realtime Database. CDNs cache and distribute your data to multiple locations worldwide, ensuring faster access for users.

3. Sharding

In cases where your database traffic is exceptionally high, consider sharding your data across multiple databases in different regions. This can help distribute the load and reduce latency for users.

Firebase Firestore

Firebase Firestore offers a more geographically distributed architecture compared to the Realtime Database. Firestore automatically replicates data across multiple regions to ensure low-latency access for users worldwide.

Firestore's multi-region support is built-in, and data synchronization happens seamlessly. When you write data to Firestore, it's automatically replicated to the nearest available region.

Here's how Firestore handles multi-region setup for you:

```
const firebaseConfig = {
  apiKey: 'YOUR_API_KEY',
  authDomain: 'your-project.firebaseapp.com',
  databaseURL: 'https://your-project.firebaseio.com',
  projectId: 'your-project',
  storageBucket: 'your-project.appspot.com',
  messagingSenderId: 'YOUR_MESSAGING_SENDER_ID',
  appId: 'YOUR_APP_ID',
  measurementId: 'YOUR_MEASUREMENT_ID',
};


firebase.initializeApp(firebaseConfig);
```

Firestore selects the appropriate region based on your users' locations, ensuring that they access data from the nearest data center. This automatic multi-region setup simplifies the process of optimizing geo-distribution for your Firestore-based applications.

In summary, Firebase offers strategies for optimizing geo-distribution in both Realtime Database and Firestore. When using Realtime Database, you can choose the right region, leverage CDNs, and consider sharding for high traffic. Firestore, on the other hand, automatically handles multi-region replication, ensuring low-latency access for users worldwide without manual configuration. Your choice between the two databases should align with your specific needs and scalability requirements.

Future Trends in Firebase Development

Firebase has evolved significantly since its inception and continues to adapt to emerging trends in app development and cloud computing. As you explore the future of Firebase development, it's essential to consider the following trends and directions that are shaping the platform's growth.

1. Serverless Computing

Serverless architecture is gaining traction in app development, and Firebase is at the forefront of this trend. Firebase Functions, a serverless compute platform, allows you to run code in response to various Firebase and HTTP events. This approach simplifies server management and scalability, making it easier to focus on application logic.

```
exports.myFunction = functions.https.onRequest((request, response) => {
  // Your code here
});
```

2. Machine Learning Integration

Firebase is integrating more machine learning capabilities to help developers create smarter and more personalized apps. Firebase Predictions is just one example, providing user behavior predictions that enable dynamic app experiences and personalized content delivery.

```
const analytics = firebase.analytics();
const predictions = analytics.getPredictions();
const predictionResult = await predictions.get('my_prediction');
```

3. Advanced Analytics and Insights

Firebase Analytics is continuously improving to provide deeper insights into user behavior. It offers more comprehensive event tracking, user segmentation, and custom metrics. Integrations with data warehouses and business intelligence tools further enhance analytics capabilities.

```
const analytics = firebase.analytics();
analytics.logEvent('purchase', { item: 'premium_membership' });
```

4. Cross-Platform Development

As cross-platform development gains popularity, Firebase provides robust support for multiple platforms, including iOS, Android, web, and Unity. Firebase's real-time data synchronization and authentication services are particularly valuable for building cross-platform apps.

```
// Firebase Authentication for multiple platforms
const auth = firebase.auth();
const user = auth.currentUser;
```

5. Enhanced Security and Compliance

Security and data privacy are top priorities for Firebase. Firebase offers features like Identity Platform for robust authentication and Realtime Database and Firestore security rules to control data access. The platform also complies with various industry standards, ensuring secure and compliant app development.

```
{
  "rules": {
    ".read": "auth != null",
    ".write": "auth != null"
  }
}
```

6. Integration with Google Cloud

Firebase is deeply integrated with Google Cloud, providing access to a wide range of cloud services. This integration allows developers to leverage Google Cloud's infrastructure, machine learning, and big data solutions seamlessly.

```
// Firebase Cloud Storage integrated with Google Cloud
const storage = firebase.storage();
```

7. Real-Time Collaboration

Firebase's real-time data synchronization capabilities are becoming essential for collaborative applications. With Firestore and the Realtime Database, you can build apps that offer real-time updates and collaboration features, such as shared documents and collaborative gaming.

```
// Real-time data synchronization with Firestore
const db = firebase.firestore();
const docRef = db.collection('documents').doc('doc1');
```

8. IoT and Edge Computing

Firebase's real-time capabilities extend to IoT and edge computing applications. You can use Firebase to build IoT solutions that require real-time data streaming and processing, making it suitable for home automation and industrial IoT applications.

```
// IoT integration with Firebase Realtime Database
const db = firebase.database();
const sensorDataRef = db.ref('sensors/sensor1');
```

In conclusion, Firebase continues to innovate and adapt to the evolving landscape of app development. With its serverless computing, machine learning integration, advanced analytics, cross-platform support, enhanced security, Google Cloud integration, real-time collaboration, and IoT capabilities, Firebase remains a powerful and versatile platform for building modern and feature-rich applications. Staying up-to-date with these trends will help you make the most of Firebase's capabilities in your future development projects.

Building a Complete Firebase Application

Planning and Designing Your Application

Building a complete Firebase application involves several crucial steps, from planning and designing your app to testing, deploying, and monitoring it. In this section, we'll explore the initial phases of creating a successful Firebase application.

1. Define Your App's Purpose and Goals

Before diving into development, you must clearly define your app's purpose and goals. Understand the problem you're solving and the target audience you're serving. Identify the core features your app should have and prioritize them based on their importance to users.

2. Sketch User Interface and User Experience (UI/UX)

Create sketches or wireframes of your app's user interface (UI) to visualize its layout and design. Consider the user experience (UX) by mapping out user flows and interactions. Tools like Figma, Sketch, or Adobe XD can help you create UI/UX prototypes.

3. Data Modeling and Database Design

Plan your data model and database schema. Decide how data will be structured and organized in Firebase Realtime Database or Firestore. Consider relationships between different data types and how they'll be queried.

4. Choose Firebase Services Wisely

Firebase offers a wide range of services, but not all of them may be relevant to your app. Select the Firebase services that align with your app's requirements. For example, if you need real-time data synchronization, choose Firestore or the Realtime Database. If authentication is crucial, integrate Firebase Authentication.

5. Set Up Firebase Project and Configuration

Create a Firebase project and configure it based on your app's requirements. Obtain the Firebase configuration settings and integrate them into your app. These settings are essential for initializing Firebase services in your code.

```
const firebaseConfig = {
  apiKey: 'YOUR_API_KEY',
  authDomain: 'YOUR_AUTH_DOMAIN',
  projectId: 'YOUR_PROJECT_ID',
  storageBucket: 'YOUR_STORAGE_BUCKET',
  messagingSenderId: 'YOUR_MESSAGING_SENDER_ID',
  appId: 'YOUR_APP_ID',
};
firebase.initializeApp(firebaseConfig);
```

6. Development Environment Setup

Set up your development environment with the necessary tools and libraries. Firebase provides SDKs for various platforms, so ensure you have the relevant SDKs installed for your chosen platforms (e.g., Android Studio for Android development or Xcode for iOS).

7. Front-end and Back-end Development

Begin developing the front-end and back-end components of your app. Implement the UI/UX designs, integrate Firebase services, and write the logic for your app's features. Use Firebase Realtime Database or Firestore to manage and retrieve data.

8. Testing and Debugging

Regularly test your app on different devices and platforms to identify and fix bugs and issues. Firebase offers tools like Firebase Test Lab for automated testing and real-device testing.

9. Security and Authentication

Implement security rules for Firebase services to ensure data privacy and access control. Configure Firebase Authentication to manage user registration and authentication securely.

10. Deployment

Prepare your app for deployment by optimizing its performance, assets, and dependencies. Use Firebase Hosting to deploy static assets, Firebase Functions for serverless backend, and Firebase Realtime Database or Firestore for data storage.

Front-end Integration and User Experience

This section explores the importance of front-end integration and creating a seamless user experience (UX) in your Firebase application.

1. Responsive Design

Ensure that your app's user interface (UI) is responsive and adapts to various screen sizes and orientations. Use CSS frameworks like Bootstrap or Materialize to simplify responsive design.

2. Real-time Updates

Leverage Firebase's real-time capabilities to provide users with live updates and notifications. Implement real-time data synchronization to keep users' data up to date without manual refreshes.

3. User Authentication

Integrate Firebase Authentication to allow users to register, sign in, and personalize their app experience. Use FirebaseUI for pre-built authentication UI components.

4. Offline Support

Implement offline support using Firebase's local caching. Users should be able to use essential app features even without an internet connection. Handle offline data synchronization and conflict resolution gracefully.

5. Error Handling

Create error handling mechanisms to provide users with clear error messages and instructions. Monitor app crashes and errors using Firebase Crashlytics for real-time error reporting.

6. User Engagement

Incorporate features that encourage user engagement, such as push notifications, in-app messaging, and personalized recommendations based on user behavior.

7. Accessibility

Ensure that your app is accessible to users with disabilities. Follow accessibility guidelines and perform testing with accessibility tools to make your app inclusive.

Testing, Deployment, and Monitoring

The final stages of building a complete Firebase application involve testing, deployment, and continuous monitoring.

1. Comprehensive Testing

Perform thorough testing, including unit tests, integration tests, and user acceptance tests. Automate testing where possible to ensure consistent and reliable results.

2. Deployment Strategy

Plan your deployment strategy carefully. Firebase Hosting simplifies static asset deployment, while Firebase Functions can be deployed as serverless functions. Implement continuous integration and delivery (CI/CD) pipelines for automated deployments.

3. Performance Optimization

Optimize your app's performance by minimizing load times, reducing resource usage, and implementing techniques like lazy loading for images and data.

4. Monitoring and Analytics

Integrate Firebase Performance Monitoring and Analytics to gain insights into your app's performance and user behavior. Monitor app crashes and errors using Firebase Crashlytics.

5. User Feedback and Improvements

Collect user feedback through in-app surveys, feedback forms, or analytics data. Use this feedback to make informed decisions for app improvements and updates.

6. Scalability

Plan for scalability from the beginning. Firebase's serverless architecture allows you to scale automatically based on demand. Monitor resource usage and adjust Firebase resources accordingly.

Case Study: A Real-World Firebase Application

To illustrate the process of building a complete Firebase application, we'll explore a real-world case study in the next section. We'll delve into the architecture, implementation, and lessons learned from a successful Firebase-powered app.

Strategies for iOS and Android Development

When building a complete Firebase application, it's crucial to consider strategies for both iOS and Android development. These strategies encompass various aspects, from development tools to user experience (UX) design and deployment. In this section, we'll explore key considerations for developing your Firebase-powered app on both iOS and Android platforms.

1. Platform-Specific Development Environments

iOS Development

For iOS development, you'll primarily use Xcode, Apple's integrated development environment (IDE). Xcode provides essential tools for building, testing, and debugging iOS apps. You'll write code in Swift or Objective-C, depending on your preference and project requirements.

Android Development

Android development typically involves using Android Studio, Google's official IDE for Android app development. Android Studio offers a robust development environment, complete with an Android emulator for testing. Kotlin is the recommended language for Android app development due to its modern features and compatibility with Java.

2. Firebase SDK Integration

Firebase provides platform-specific SDKs for iOS and Android, making it seamless to integrate Firebase services into your app.

To integrate Firebase into your iOS app, you'll use the Firebase iOS SDK. Add Firebase to your Xcode project by including the Firebase configuration file (GoogleService-Info.plist). You can then initialize Firebase services and use Firebase pods for features like Firestore, Authentication, and Realtime Database.

```swift
import Firebase

// Initialize Firebase
FirebaseApp.configure()
```

Android Integration

For Android, you'll include the Firebase configuration file (google-services.json) in your Android Studio project. Add the Firebase SDK dependencies to your app-level build.gradle file. Initialize Firebase in your app's entry point (usually the Application class).

```java
// In your Application class
import com.google.firebase.FirebaseApp;

// Initialize Firebase
FirebaseApp.initializeApp(this);
```

3. User Interface and User Experience (UI/UX) Design

Cross-Platform UI/UX

Consider using cross-platform UI/UX design libraries like Flutter (for Dart) or React Native (for JavaScript) to create consistent UI across both iOS and Android. These frameworks allow you to share a significant portion of your codebase and UI components.

Platform-Specific Design

While cross-platform development can save time, it's essential to adhere to platform-specific design guidelines. iOS follows Human Interface Guidelines (HIG), while Android follows Material Design. Adapt your app's UI to provide a native look and feel on each platform.

4. User Authentication

Firebase Authentication offers platform-specific UI components to handle user registration, sign-in, and profile management. Ensure a seamless authentication experience for users on both iOS and Android.

iOS Authentication

Use FirebaseUI for iOS to provide a consistent authentication UI on iOS devices. Customize the UI to match your app's design while maintaining a user-friendly experience.

FirebaseUI for Android simplifies the implementation of authentication features on Android. Customize the appearance and behavior to align with your app's aesthetics.

5. Testing and Debugging

Cross-Platform Testing

Utilize cross-platform testing frameworks like Appium or Detox to automate UI testing across both iOS and Android. These tools allow you to write tests once and run them on both platforms.

Platform-Specific Testing

Perform platform-specific testing to ensure your app functions correctly on each platform. Emulators and simulators are invaluable for testing on iOS and Android devices.

6. App Deployment

App Store Submission

Prepare your app for submission to the Apple App Store and Google Play Store. Follow the respective guidelines and review processes for each platform. Be aware of platform-specific app submission requirements.

Over-the-Air (OTA) Updates

Consider using Firebase App Distribution for distributing pre-release versions of your app to testers. Firebase makes it easy to send OTA updates, collect feedback, and monitor app stability.

7. Performance Optimization

Optimize your app's performance for both iOS and Android devices. Monitor memory usage, CPU consumption, and network requests on each platform. Leverage Firebase Performance Monitoring to identify performance bottlenecks.

iOS Optimization

Instruments, Apple's performance profiling tool, can help you identify and resolve performance issues on iOS devices. Optimize code execution and memory management for a smooth user experience.

Android Optimization

Use Android Profiler in Android Studio to profile your app's performance on Android devices. Address issues related to CPU, memory, and rendering to ensure optimal performance.

8. User Feedback and Continuous Improvement

Collect user feedback on both platforms to drive app improvements. Firebase allows you to gather feedback through in-app surveys and analytics. Regularly release updates and enhancements to keep users engaged.

9. Cross-Platform Integration

Ensure that your Firebase app seamlessly integrates with cross-platform features like Firebase Realtime Database or Firestore. Implement data synchronization and real-time updates consistently on both iOS and Android.

10. Platform-Specific Features

Consider adding platform-specific features or optimizations when necessary. Some features may perform better or offer unique capabilities on one platform over the other. Tailor your app accordingly to provide the best user experience.

By following these strategies for iOS and Android development, you can create a Firebase-powered app that delivers a consistent, high-quality experience on both major mobile platforms. Prioritize user satisfaction, performance, and seamless integration to ensure your app's success.

Front-end Integration and User Experience

Front-end integration and user experience (UX) are critical components of building a complete Firebase application. In this section, we will explore the importance of a well-designed front end and how to integrate Firebase services seamlessly into your app to enhance user experience.

1. Designing a User-Centric Front End

A user-centric front end is essential for creating a positive user experience. Consider the following design principles:

- **Intuitive Navigation**: Ensure that users can easily navigate through your app. Use clear and straightforward menu structures and navigation patterns.

- **Responsive Design**: Design your app to work well on various screen sizes and orientations. Implement responsive layouts and adapt to different devices.

- **Consistency**: Maintain consistency in design elements, such as colors, fonts, and button styles, to create a unified and familiar look and feel.

- **Accessibility**: Make your app accessible to users with disabilities. Follow accessibility guidelines and provide alternative text for images and proper labeling for interactive elements.

- **Performance**: Optimize front-end performance by minimizing loading times and using lazy loading techniques for assets.

2. Firebase Authentication Integration

Integrating Firebase Authentication into your front end is crucial for user registration, sign-in, and profile management. Firebase offers easy-to-use libraries for web and mobile apps.

- **Web Integration**: Use the Firebase JavaScript SDK for web applications. FirebaseUI for web provides pre-built UI components for authentication, making it simple to add sign-in and registration forms to your web app.

```javascript
// Initialize Firebase
var firebaseConfig = {
  apiKey: "YOUR_API_KEY",
  authDomain: "YOUR_AUTH_DOMAIN",
  projectId: "YOUR_PROJECT_ID",
  storageBucket: "YOUR_STORAGE_BUCKET",
  messagingSenderId: "YOUR_MESSAGING_SENDER_ID",
  appId: "YOUR_APP_ID"
};

firebase.initializeApp(firebaseConfig);

// Create an instance of FirebaseUI
var ui = new firebaseui.auth.AuthUI(firebase.auth());

// Configure FirebaseUI options
var uiConfig = {
  signInSuccessUrl: '/',
  signInOptions: [
    firebase.auth.EmailAuthProvider.PROVIDER_ID,
    firebase.auth.GoogleAuthProvider.PROVIDER_ID,
    // Add other authentication providers as needed
  ],
  // Other configuration options
};

// Start the FirebaseUI authentication process
ui.start('#firebaseui-auth-container', uiConfig);
```

- **Mobile Integration**: For mobile apps, use the Firebase Authentication SDKs for Android and iOS. These SDKs provide ready-to-use components for user authentication within your mobile app.

3. Realtime Data Integration

If your app requires real-time data synchronization, Firebase Realtime Database and Firestore are excellent choices. Both offer real-time updates and seamless integration with front-end frameworks.

- **Web Integration**: Use the Firebase JavaScript SDK to integrate Realtime Database or Firestore into your web app. You can subscribe to data changes and update the UI in real time.

```javascript
// Realtime Database example
var db = firebase.database();
var ref = db.ref('your-data-path');

ref.on('value', function(snapshot) {
  // Update the UI with new data
  var data = snapshot.val();
  // Update the UI elements
});
```

- **Mobile Integration**: Integrate Firebase Realtime Database or Firestore into your mobile app using the Firebase SDKs for Android and iOS. Implement listeners to receive real-time updates when data changes occur.

4. Cloud Functions Integration

Firebase Cloud Functions allow you to run serverless code in response to various events. You can use them to perform server-side logic, such as sending notifications, processing data, and more.

- **Web Integration**: Invoke Firebase Cloud Functions from your web app using the Firebase JavaScript SDK. You can call functions and handle responses asynchronously.

```javascript
// Call a Firebase Cloud Function
var callFunction = firebase.functions().httpsCallable('yourFunctionName');

callFunction({ /* data to send */ })
  .then(function(result) {
    // Handle the function's response
  })
  .catch(function(error) {
    // Handle errors
  });
```

- **Mobile Integration**: On mobile platforms, you can use Firebase SDKs for Android and iOS to call Cloud Functions. Handle the function calls and responses accordingly within your app.

Integrate Firebase Analytics into your front end to gain insights into user behavior and app performance. Firebase also allows you to collect user feedback through surveys and monitor crash reports.

- **Web Integration**: Use the Firebase JavaScript SDK to log events and track user interactions in your web app. Customize analytics to gather specific data that aligns with your app's objectives.

```javascript
// Log a custom event
firebase.analytics().logEvent('custom_event', { param1: 'value1', param2: 'value2' });
```

- **Mobile Integration**: For mobile apps, include the Firebase Analytics SDK for Android and iOS. Track user engagement, retention, and conversion rates to make data-driven decisions.

Ensure that your front-end design is responsive, adapting to various screen sizes and orientations. Test your app on different devices and browsers to ensure cross-platform compatibility.

- **Responsive Layouts**: Use CSS frameworks like Bootstrap or CSS Grid to create responsive layouts that adjust to different screen sizes seamlessly.

- **Cross-Browser Testing**: Test your web app on major browsers, including Chrome, Firefox, Safari, and Edge, to identify and resolve compatibility issues.

Consider adding progressive web app features to your web application, allowing users to install your app on their devices and use it offline. Implement service workers for caching and offline access.

Prioritize user-centric testing to ensure your app's front-end functionality and usability. Conduct usability testing, gather user feedback, and iterate on your design and user experience based on user insights.

By integrating Firebase services seamlessly into your app's front end, you can create a user-friendly and engaging experience for your audience. Focus on responsive design, authentication, real-time data, and analytics to build a complete Firebase application that meets user expectations.

Testing, Deployment, and Monitoring

Testing, deployment, and monitoring are crucial phases in the development lifecycle of a Firebase application. In this section, we'll explore the best practices for ensuring your app's reliability, performance, and stability.

1. Testing Your Firebase Application

Testing is an integral part of app development. Firebase offers various testing tools and practices to help you ensure the quality and reliability of your app.

- **Unit Testing**: Write unit tests for your code using testing frameworks like Jest for JavaScript or JUnit for Android. Firebase provides the Firebase Testing Emulator Suite to simulate Firebase services for testing.

```javascript
// Example of unit testing a Firebase function
const functions = require('firebase-functions');
const admin = require('firebase-admin');
admin.initializeApp();

test('Function should return the correct value', () => {
  const data = { key: 'value' };
  const context = { /* context object */ };
  const result = myFunction(data, context);
  expect(result).toBe('expectedValue');
});
```

- **Integration Testing**: Perform integration tests to check how different components of your app work together. Firebase Emulator Suite can be useful for emulating Firebase services during integration testing.

- **UI Testing**: For mobile apps, consider UI testing frameworks like Espresso for Android or XCTest for iOS to automate UI tests. Firebase Test Lab provides cloud-based testing on real devices for Android and iOS.

2. Continuous Integration and Continuous Deployment (CI/CD)

Implement a CI/CD pipeline to automate testing, building, and deploying your Firebase app. Popular CI/CD services like Travis CI, CircleCI, or GitHub Actions can be used to set up automated workflows.

- **Version Control**: Use a version control system like Git to manage your codebase. Host it on platforms like GitHub, GitLab, or Bitbucket.

- **Automated Builds**: Set up automated build processes that compile your code, run tests, and generate deployment artifacts.

- **Continuous Deployment**: Configure your CI/CD pipeline to deploy to Firebase Hosting, Cloud Functions, or other Firebase services automatically when changes are pushed to a specific branch.

3. Monitoring App Performance

Monitoring app performance is essential to identify and resolve issues proactively. Firebase offers tools for real-time monitoring and error tracking.

- **Firebase Performance Monitoring**: Use Firebase Performance Monitoring to gain insights into your app's performance. Monitor response times, network requests, and custom traces.

```
// Log a custom trace
const trace = firebase.performance().trace('custom_trace');
trace.start();
// Code to be traced
trace.stop();
```

- **Error Tracking**: Firebase Crashlytics provides real-time error tracking for mobile apps. Receive crash reports and analyze error details to quickly resolve issues.

- **Analytics Monitoring**: Regularly review Firebase Analytics to understand user behavior, identify bottlenecks, and optimize your app accordingly.

4. Scaling and Load Testing

Ensure that your Firebase app can handle increased loads as it grows in popularity. Perform load testing to identify performance bottlenecks and capacity limits.

- **Firebase Blaze Plan**: Consider upgrading to the Blaze plan, which allows you to customize your usage and handle higher loads. Monitor your usage and billing closely.

- **Load Testing Tools**: Use load testing tools like Apache JMeter, Gatling, or Locust to simulate heavy traffic and measure your app's performance under stress.

- **Database Scaling**: Optimize your database design and security rules to handle more concurrent users. Consider Firestore's auto-scaling capabilities.

5. Security Audits

Regularly audit your Firebase app's security to identify vulnerabilities and ensure data protection.

- **Firebase Security Rules**: Review and update Firebase Security Rules to enforce access control and protect your data from unauthorized access.

- **Data Encryption**: Use Firebase Authentication and Firestore's server-side security to ensure data encryption and protect user information.

6. Backups and Data Recovery

Implement backup and data recovery strategies to protect your app's data in case of unexpected data loss or outages.

- **Firestore Data Exports**: Periodically export Firestore data using Firebase CLI or scheduled Cloud Functions. Store backups securely in a different location.

- **Realtime Database Backups**: Enable automated backups for the Realtime Database through Firebase Console or Firebase CLI.

7. Disaster Recovery Plan

Develop a disaster recovery plan outlining steps to follow in case of a major outage or data breach. Ensure that your team is prepared to react swiftly and effectively.

- **Incident Response Team**: Form an incident response team with defined roles and responsibilities.

- **Communication Plan**: Establish a communication plan to notify users, stakeholders, and relevant authorities in case of a breach or significant outage.

- **Data Restore Procedures**: Document data restore procedures and practice them to minimize downtime in a disaster scenario.

By following these best practices in testing, deployment, and monitoring, you can ensure that your Firebase application is robust, performs well under various conditions, and remains secure and reliable throughout its lifecycle. Regularly revisit and update these practices as your app evolves to meet changing user needs and industry standards.

Future Trends in Firebase Development

Firebase has been at the forefront of mobile and web app development, offering a comprehensive suite of tools and services to developers. As technology continues to evolve, it's essential to stay informed about future trends and advancements in Firebase development. In this section, we'll explore some potential future trends that may shape the Firebase ecosystem.

1. Integration with Emerging Technologies

Firebase is likely to integrate more seamlessly with emerging technologies such as augmented reality (AR), virtual reality (VR), and Internet of Things (IoT). Developers can expect enhanced support for building applications that leverage these technologies while benefiting from Firebase's real-time data synchronization and serverless architecture.

```javascript
// Example of AR-based app using Firebase for real-time data updates
const arApp = firebase.initializeApp(config);
const arDatabase = arApp.database();
```

2. Machine Learning and AI Integration

Machine learning and artificial intelligence are becoming increasingly prevalent in app development. Firebase's existing capabilities in machine learning, like Firebase ML Kit, may evolve to provide even more advanced tools for integrating AI-powered features into apps.

```javascript
// Example of integrating Firebase ML Kit for image recognition
const imageRecognizer = firebase.ml().imageRecognizer();
const image = /* Image data */;
imageRecognizer.processImage(image)
  .then((result) => {
    console.log('Recognition result:', result);
  });
```

3. Enhanced Real-Time Collaboration

Firebase's real-time database and Firestore have been instrumental in building collaborative applications. Future developments might focus on enhancing real-time collaboration features, enabling developers to create even more interactive and collaborative apps.

```javascript
// Example of a collaborative document editing app using Firebase
const collaborativeApp = firebase.initializeApp(config);
const collaborativeDatabase = collaborativeApp.firestore();
```

4. Improved Serverless Functions

Firebase Cloud Functions, which allow developers to run serverless code in response to events, are likely to see improvements in terms of scalability, performance, and developer experience. This will make it easier to build complex serverless architectures.

```javascript
// Example of a Firebase Cloud Function
exports.myFunction = functions.firestore
  .document('myCollection/{documentId}')
  .onCreate((snapshot, context) => {
    // Function logic here
  });
```

5. Expanded Analytics Capabilities

Firebase Analytics may offer more extensive insights and data analysis capabilities, allowing developers to gain deeper insights into user behavior and app performance. This can help developers make data-driven decisions for app optimization.

```javascript
// Example of custom analytics event tracking
firebase.analytics().logEvent('custom_event', {
  parameter1: 'value1',
  parameter2: 'value2',
});
```

6. Cross-Platform Development

Cross-platform app development is on the rise, and Firebase is likely to continue supporting and enhancing its features for building apps that run on multiple platforms, including web, iOS, and Android.

```
// Example of cross-platform development with Firebase
const webApp = firebase.initializeApp(webConfig);
const iosApp = firebase.initializeApp(iosConfig);
const androidApp = firebase.initializeApp(androidConfig);
```

7. Enhanced Security and Compliance

As data privacy regulations evolve, Firebase is expected to provide more comprehensive tools for securing user data and ensuring compliance with various privacy laws, such as GDPR and CCPA.

```
// Example of Firebase security rules for user data protection
service cloud.firestore {
  match /databases/{database}/documents {
    match /users/{userId} {
      allow read, write: if request.auth.uid == userId;
    }
  }
}
```

8. Community Contributions and Open Source Development

Firebase's vibrant developer community is likely to continue contributing to open-source Firebase extensions, libraries, and tools. Developers can expect to see more community-driven projects that enhance Firebase's capabilities.

```
// Example of using a community-contributed Firebase extension
const extension = firebase.ext().getExtension('community_extension');
```

These potential future trends in Firebase development showcase the platform's adaptability and commitment to meeting the evolving needs of developers and users. As Firebase continues to evolve, staying informed about these trends will help developers make the most of Firebase's powerful features and capabilities.